God Hears Her
FOR GIRLS

90 FAITH-BUILDING DEVOTIONS

Our Daily Bread
Publishing™

Requests for permission to quote from this book should be directed to: Permissions Department, Our Daily Bread Publishing, PO Box 3566, Grand Rapids, MI 49501, or contact us by email at permissionsdept@odb.org.

Scripture quotations, unless otherwise indicated, are taken from the Holy Bible, New Living Translation, copyright © 1996, 2004, 2015 by Tyndale House Foundation. Used by permission of Tyndale House Publishers, Inc., Carol Stream, Illinois 60188. All rights reserved.

Scripture quotations marked NIV are taken from the Holy Bible, New International Version®, NIV®. Copyright © 1973, 1978, 1984, 2011 by Biblica, Inc.™ Used by permission of Zondervan. All rights reserved worldwide. www.zondervan.com.

Scripture quotations marked NIrV are taken from the Holy Bible, New International Reader's Version®, NIrV® Copyright © 1995, 1996, 1998 by Biblica, Inc.™ Used by permission of Zondervan. All rights reserved worldwide. www.zondervan.com

Scripture quotations marked MSG are taken from *The Message.* Copyright © 1993, 2002, 2018 by Eugene H. Peterson. Used by permission of NavPress. All rights reserved. Represented by Tyndale House Publishers, a Division of Tyndale House Ministries.

Interior design by Patti Brinks

Library of Congress Cataloging-in-Publication Data Available

Printed in the United States of America
21 22 23 24 25 26 27 28 / 8 7 6 5 4 3 2 1

Introduction

This book is for girls like you. Girls with brave hearts. Girls with adventurous spirits. Girls who think big. Most of all? It's for girls who love God with *everything* they've got! That means the God of the universe is their friend and they listen to Him (check out "How Can I Be Friends with God?" page 186, if you want to learn more about having a personal relationship with God).

Before we begin, God wants you to know something really important. It's a message that He'll share with you again and again as you read *God Hears Her for Girls*. You're special to Him. So, whatever you face—and no matter how you feel—you can run to Him. On your best days when your heart is *bursting* with joy. On your worst ones too: those days you just want to hide. No matter if you're incredibly excited or sad, hopeful or scared, He wants to hear *it all*. *Everything* that's on your heart.

God Hears Her for Girls can help you talk to God. As you read each devotion—with its fun story, Bible verse, and discussion question—you can share your thoughts and feelings with the King of the universe. (Maybe even have a journal ready, so you can journal your thoughts to Him too.) Here's the thing: Don't just read the stories. *Listen in* with your heart. Because God has important things to tell you! About His amazing plans for you. About your unique role in His unbreakable, forever kingdom. And about all the gifts He's specially given to you.

So settle in to your comfiest chair. (Maybe wear your coziest pj's too.) Then open up the first day's devotion with excitement, knowing you're about to have a conversation with God.

God Hears Her
FOR GIRLS

1

FOR A WARRIOR LIKE YOU

Finally, be strong in the Lord and in his mighty power. Put on the full armor of God, so that you can take your stand against the devil's schemes.

Ephesians 6:10–11 (NIV)

Hi there, strong warrior! Yes, that's you. Did you know that God is calling you to fight the forces of evil, meaning Satan and his armies? It's true. You have an epic mission, but here's a little secret: you're not carrying out your assignment alone. You couldn't, in fact, do this alone. Not ever. Your King Jesus will win this war, but He's asking you to bravely follow Him into battle.

So, are you ready to suit up? First, put on your protective gear: your belt of truth, your breastplate of righteousness, your helmet of salvation, and your shield of faith. When the arrows from the Enemy start flying at you (often in the form of lies), you can put up your shield of faith. Those arrows will boomerang right off, unable to hurt you. Whoa.

Your deadliest weapon? The sword of the Spirit. You can attack your Enemy with this incredibly powerful sword that is God's words: His words in the Bible and those He shares with you in prayer.

Finally, don't forget your shoes. With good shoes, you can run at top speeds, sharing God's love with everyone you know.

Now that you're dressed, you're ready to do battle.

What's your favorite spiritual weapon? Why?

Jesus, help me suit up and get ready for the fight against the Enemy. Thanks for going before me and always protecting me!

You can read about the war against our Enemy in Ephesians 6:10–18.

2
GOD'S UNBREAKABLE KINGDOM

**Put God's kingdom first. Do what he wants
you to do. Then all those things will also be
given to you.**

Matthew 6:33 (NIrV)

Have you ever watched *Frozen I* or *II*, in which spunky
princesses Anna and Elsa, along with everyone's favorite
snowman sidekick—Olaf—take us on adventures as they
learn to rule their kingdom?

Except in movies with singing snowmen, we don't often hear the
word *kingdom*. The moment you accept Jesus into your heart,
though, you belong to a new one. Yes, really. In this kingdom, you
answer to a higher power than your school principal, the president,
or—even—your parents. (It's hard to believe.) You see, Jesus is

your King. He's mightier than any government, king, or queen on Earth or in the entire universe (including spiritual kingdoms too!). One day, the Bible says, all leaders—including your principal—will bow down to your King of Kings. Whoa.

Wait, there's more! Did you know that your King is a rule-breaker? It's true. The rules in His kingdom are flipped upside down, topsy-turvy even. In his kingdom, leaders don't get special treatment. Nope. They're the first to serve! In his kingdom, you love your enemies, not just your friends. Here, you put others—not yourself—first.

The most incredible news? In God's kingdom, you get to live forever, with the King who loves you with everything He's got.

What's the most awesome thing about God's kingdom?

Jesus, thanks for Your unbreakable, unshakeable, upside-down kingdom. I love that I get to live forever with You as my King.

You can read about God's unbreakable kingdom in Mark 10:13–16.

3

KING'S DAUGHTER

The LORD your God is with you, the Mighty
Warrior who saves. He will take great
delight in you; in his love he will . . . rejoice
over you with singing.

Zephaniah 3:17 (NIV)

*H*ow do you describe yourself? Maybe you talk about your *personality*, how you're funny, shy, or spunky. Or, about the *things you do*, like playing piano or soccer. Or about *what you love*, like a favorite song or show. These are *great* ways to describe who you are.

Your Creator has some very important things to share with you about your identity too: First, you just so happen to be the daughter of the King of the universe. (That means you're royal.) You are also *beloved*, a fancy—even old-fashioned—word with a big meaning: Your heavenly Father is crazy about you. He loves your brave heart, your curious mind, your energy. He treasures your smile and your strength. Everything about you makes your Father's heart burst with joy.

He even sings lullabies over you in heaven (Zephaniah 3:17)!

Sometimes people will try to tear you down. Be brave enough to tune in to your Father, who will remind you of who you really are: a beloved, royal daughter of the King.

How do you describe yourself?

Jesus, sometimes it's easy to forget who I really am. Help me remember that I'm treasured and loved by You.

You can read how God sings over you in heaven in Zephaniah 3:14–17.

4

THE WEAVER KING

**The LORD says, "I will rescue those who love me.
I will protect those who trust in my name. When
they call on me, I will answer; I will be with
them in trouble. I will rescue and honor them."**

Psalm 91:14–15

There's a legend about a king who wanted the most beautiful wall hangings in his palace. To everyone's surprise, the king hired kids for the job.

On the day of the children's arrival, the king revealed a secret to them, "Before I became emperor, I was a weaver.

"If you ever need help, you can always come to me."

The following weeks and months, the girls and boys worked non-stop, but their silk kept tangling, their fabric ruined by the holes at the center of their designs. None of their tapestries were worthy of a king's palace.

Except for one girl's. One tiny girl kept mysteriously churning out masterpieces of gold and red thread, full of images of tigers and unicorns, almost as if by magic.

Dumbfounded, they finally asked her the secret to her success.

She smiled and said simply, "Every morning, I go to the emperor and ask him for help."

The king had offered to help—and only one of them had taken him up on his offer.

The King of the universe gives you the very same offer. No matter the time or place, God promises to be available to you. (Helping His kids is one of His favorite things.)

Remember your King's door is wide open.

What do you need help with right now? Talk to your King about it.

Jesus, You're pretty busy, but You promise that Your door is wide open—that I can go to you at any time. That blows my mind!

You can read about God's awesome help in Psalm 91:11–16.

5

MAKE MY BROWN EYES BLUE

For you created my inmost being; you knit me together in my mother's womb. I praise you because I am fearfully and wonderfully made; your works are wonderful, I know that full well

Psalm 139:13–14 (NIV)

Amy Carmichael was born with *gorgeous* brown eyes. But Carmichael, who later became a famous missionary in India, wanted blue eyes. She even prayed for God to change her eye color from brown to blue!

Here's the amazing thing: When she arrived in India, Carmichael discovered most everyone had dark eyes—just like her! Because

she had dark eyes, Amy was accepted more quickly into her new community.

God designed Amy Carmichael—and all of us—purposely. Our God is a Master Artist. When God created you, He lovingly mixed together his rainbow of hues to create the exact color of your gorgeous eyes. He selected the texture—straight, wavy, or curly—of your hair. He thoughtfully built out your curious mind, giving you amazing talents and brilliant abilities too. Nothing escaped you Creator's attention when He lovingly crafted you.

You are your Creator's masterpiece.

⸙⸙⸙⸙⸙⸙⸙

What do you like about yourself?

Jesus, You created me beautifully and specially—I am Your masterpiece!

You can read how God created you uniquely in Psalm 139:13–18.

6
WALKING IN GOD'S DIRT

One day as Jesus was walking along the shore of the Sea of Galilee, he saw Simon and his brother Andrew throwing a net into the water, for they fished for a living. Jesus called out to them, "Come, follow me, and I will show you how to fish for people!" And they left their nets at once and followed him.

Mark 1:16–18

*S*chool was different in Jesus's time. You'd move out of your parents' house and move in with your teacher (called the "rabbi").

You'd also follow your teacher around—literally. There's a funny saying about this; it's something like, Students walk around in their rabbi's dirt. That's because students walked behind their teachers so closely that the dirt their teachers kicked up would settle on them!

You may be asking, What's the point of all of this? As a student—a *disciple*—you didn't want to just memorize facts. Nope. You wanted to become *exactly* like your teacher. That's why the disciples left everything—including their families—to follow Jesus.

Jesus calls us to be His disciples too. So, listen to Him and obey what He says. By following in Jesus's footsteps, you can walk in "God's dirt"—becoming just like your Rabbi.

⚶⚶⚶⚶

What do you think about school in Jesus's time?

Jesus, help me walk in Your dirt—listening to what You say and loving others as You do. I want to become just like You! Please show me how.

You can read about Jesus choosing the disciples in Mark 1:16–20.

7

REALLY, REALLY HUNGRY ... AND TEMPTED

Jesus answered, "It is written: 'Man shall not live on bread alone, but on every word that comes from the mouth of God.'"

Matthew 4:4

Have you ever been so hungry that you could've eaten a mountain of fries, eight slices of pizza, and maybe even a slice of ice cream cake too?

When we're hungry, we'd do almost anything to fill our bellies.

Today's Bible story tells us Jesus was really, really hungry too. He had been fasting forty days. (Fasting is whenever you take a break from meals, or, even worse—chocolate—to focus on your friendship with God.) Satan decided that forty days into Jesus's fast was

the *perfect* time to offer Jesus a temptation in the form of freshly baked bread. Pretty rotten, right?

The next time you're tempted, remember this: Jesus knows *exactly* what you're going through. How it feels to be tempted when you're struggling or just really, really hungry. Even at one of His toughest moments ever, Jesus told the Enemy, "No thanks."

Because Jesus already defeated Satan, He'll give you His amazing power to say "No!" to temptation too.

Have you ever been tempted when you were really, really hungry, . . . or tired, . . . or alone?

Jesus, you know what it's like to be tempted. Help me to do the right thing whenever I'm tempted.

You can read about the time Jesus was really hungry . . . and tempted in Matthew 4:1–11.

8
LIKE A CHAMPION

Everyone who competes in the games goes into strict training. They do it to get a crown that will not last, but we do it to get a crown that will last forever.

1 Corinthians 9:25 (NIV)

*H*ave you ever watched Simone Biles compete at the Olympics? The incredibly talented gymnast has won more medals than any other American gymnast. To go for the gold, Biles doesn't just show up at the Olympics without practicing and expect to win. No way! She practices at least six hours a day. Imagine how many handsprings, round-offs, and vaults that is in a year: wow.

In the same way Biles gets ready for the Olympics, you're to train your heart and mind like a champion. You see, God wants you to build up your spiritual muscles. How? As an Olympic athlete is physically strong, God can make your heart and mind strong. If you ask Him for help, He'll give you the strength to make good choices, and the amazing power to say no to things that aren't good for you. So, listen to Him when you pray. Do the right things. And read God's Word, the Bible. The Bible says there's even a prize for God's very own champions—"a crown that will last forever" (1 Corinthians 9:25).

With Jesus's help, you'll grow a courageous heart.

How can you build your spiritual muscles this week?

Jesus, help me to build up my spiritual muscles and grow powerful in You!

You can read about becoming a champion in 1 Corinthians 9:24–27.

9

GOD'S GREATEST TREASURE

Don't store up treasures here on earth, where moths eat them and rust destroys them, and where thieves break in and steal. Store your treasures in heaven, where moths and rust cannot destroy, and thieves do not break in and steal.

Matthew 6:19–20

In the ancient kingdom of Dacia, gold was everywhere. Emperors greedily tried to get ahold of all that gold. Especially jealous were they of King Decebalus, the ruler of Dacia. Being a ruler in a kingdom full of gold made the king a very rich man.

King Decebalus wanted to keep it that way—so he came up with a sneaky plan: Next to his palace was a river, and the king forced the river to change direction. (Kings did anything they wanted back then!) Then, sneakily, he unlocked his trove of gold from the palace and carried it to the now dry riverbed. There, he buried his

treasure. Then, the king made the river flow *just* as it did before. Hiding his big secret.

Only after the king died was the secret revealed: that piles of gold lay hidden at the bottom of the river! Whoa.

This is a story about a king obsessed with keeping his treasure all to himself.

Unlike this king, our King—our heavenly Father—gives freely of His treasures. His greatest treasure? His only Son. The Son He loved with all His might: "For this is how God loved the world: He gave his one and only Son, so that everyone who believes in him will not perish but have eternal life" (John 3:16).

A generous Gift-Giver, God gave up His most precious Treasure—Jesus—to give us the gift of life forever with Him. Have you accepted His free gift?

Have you chosen to love God with your whole heart? You can make that decision right now!

Jesus, You are God's greatest Treasure. I believe that You died on the cross for my sins and came back to life again! I'm sorry for my sins. Please come into my heart and life, and be my King and my Friend. I want to live forever with You. In Jesus's name, amen.

You can read about treasure in Matthew 6:19–21.

10
STINKY FEET

So [Jesus] got up from the table, took off his robe, wrapped a towel around his waist, and poured water into a basin. Then he began to wash the disciples' feet, drying them with the towel he had around him.

John 13:4–5

*H*ave you ever been running around in your tennis shoes all day? If you have, then you know what happens to feet after they've been outside for a long time—they stink.

Jesus's disciples had a day like that, a long day of walking everywhere. Guess what? They had smelly feet too. The unexpected thing, though? Jesus volunteered to wash their feet (and He knew just how stinky their feet would be).

Just as we would have, the disciple Peter protested.

"No," he cried out to Jesus, "you will never ever wash my feet!" (John 13:8). You see, Peter knew Jesus was a king. And kings don't wash stinky feet. But Peter missed something important. Jesus rules an upside-down kingdom. A kingdom in which important people forget special privileges. Instead, they're the first to serve.

So, will you follow Jesus's example? In God's kingdom, we're called to humbly serve, even if the job is a little bit stinky.

How can you serve those around you today?

Jesus, I can't believe You washed stinky feet! Help me follow Your example by serving others, even when the work isn't glamorous.

You can read the story of Jesus washing stinky feet in John 13:1–17.

11

CALLED TO BE COURAGEOUS

God blesses those who are persecuted for doing right, for the Kingdom of Heaven is theirs.

Matthew 5:10

*I*n her bedroom was a secret room—a fake wall opening up to a small compartment. Inside it, up to six people could hide. During the Holocaust, Corrie ten Boom and her family saved eight hundred Jews and other refugees, hiding them in that small room and in safe homes across Europe.

Corrie ten Boom risked her life to do the right thing. For her brave actions, the Nazis sent her to a concentration camp. Even in one of the darkest places, God shined brightly in Corrie ten Boom, because of her, many of the prisoners started a relationship with

Jesus inside the camp. When released, ten Boom shared her story of faith and courage around the world.

As was true for Corrie ten Boom, Christ-followers around the world face persecution for living out their faith today, especially in the places where following Jesus is against the law. The Bible says, "God blesses those who are persecuted for doing right, for the Kingdom of Heaven is theirs" (Matthew 5:10).

Let's pray for our brothers and sisters facing persecution. And may we always be ready to stand up for others, just like Corrie ten Boom.

How was Corrie ten Boom called to be courageous? How are you being called to be courageous too?

Jesus, watch over the people all around the world risking their lives to follow You, especially those living in countries where sharing Your story is against the law! Help them be bold in sharing Your love, even in the hardest places.

You can read about standing up for your faith in Matthew 5:10–12.

12

THANK-YOU LETTER

Give my greetings to Priscilla and Aquila, my co-workers in the ministry of Christ Jesus. In fact, they once risked their lives for me. I am thankful to them, and so are all the Gentile churches.

Romans 16:3–4

*C*an you think of someone you're very thankful for? Maybe they helped you out or are just a special person in your life? Here's a fun idea: write a thank-you letter, telling this person what they did to make you so thankful for him or her. Then, meet with this amazing person—whether virtually or in person—reading your letter out loud to them. They'll love it. (You will too!)

Around the world, in a whole movement of thank-you-note writing, thousands of people have read their letters aloud to their special people—and the people on the receiving end were incredibly encouraged.

The Bible is full of letters, and the authors often remember to thank their good friends too. Here's a great example: In his letter to the church in Rome, Paul thanked his close friends Priscilla and Aquila for how brave they were to risk their lives for him—he said not only he, but all the churches were thankful for their courageous missionary work (Romans 16:3–4).

So, who are you going to thank today? Because you're not only going to make his or her day—but yours too!

Who do you want to write your thank-you letter to? You can start writing it now.

Jesus, there are so many things to be grateful for—and sometimes I forget about them. Remind me to be thankful for the things You've blessed me with, no matter if they're big or small!

You can read Paul's letter of thanks to his friends in Romans 16.

13

BERNIE THE SAINT BERNARD

The name of the LORD is like a strong tower.
Godly people run to it and are safe.

Proverbs 18:10 (NIrV)

*B*ernie the Saint Bernard believed he was still a puppy. You should know, though, that he was enormous, furry—weighing almost two-hundred pounds! (Truthfully, Bernie looked more like a grizzly bear than a dog.) One day, Bernie got loose in the park—just as Jess and her little brother Jack were walking into the park's entrance.

Bernie saw Jack. Little Jack eyed Bernie.

To the dog (who thought he was still a puppy), Jack looked like the *perfect* playmate. To Jack, Bernie looked like a big bear. So, when Bernie began running toward his newest best friend, you can guess what Jack did, right? He took off!

It was impossible for Jack to outrun big Bernie. So, his big sister yelled out, "Jack, run back to me!" He ran into Jess's arms, just in time, before Bernie caught him!

There are moments when God calls out to us, "Run to Me!" Something scary is at our heels. We can't shake it. We're too afraid to turn and face the trouble on our own. But here's the thing: we aren't on our own. God is there, ready to help and protect us. Always. We can turn away from whatever scares us and move in His direction. The Bible says, "The name of the Lord is like a strong tower. Godly people run to it and are safe" (Proverbs 18:10 NIrV).

So, whenever you need help? Run to Him.

ﬆﬆﬆﬆﬆ

Have you ever seen a Saint Bernard like Bernie?

Jesus, whenever I'm scared or in trouble, help me run to You.

You can read about how God protects you in Psalm 18:1–3.

14
MEET SHREK

The LORD is my shepherd; I have all that I need

Psalm 23:1

Shrek the sheep got lost. For six years, the sheep from New Zealand was missing from his flock. For those six years, his fleece never stopped growing. The more it grew, the wilder he looked. His coat was so long, in fact, that the person who found him high on a mountaintop didn't even know he was a sheep!

Shrek had to be carried down the mountain because his fleece was so heavy (sixty pounds) that he couldn't walk on his own! Don't worry: they sheared Shrek, so he could walk like a normal sheep again. Shrek is a picture of what can happen to a sheep separated from its shepherd.

Jesus talks a lot about sheep. In fact, He calls himself the Good Shepherd (John 10:11), and He calls us His sheep. Many times, we act like Shrek the sheep. We want to do our own thing, so we wander off and stop listening to our Good Shepherd. But our choices can weigh us down—like Shrek's sixty-pound fleece!

How do you stay away from that kind of trouble? Stay close to your Good Shepherd, Jesus.

Have you ever made a choice that weighed you down like Shrek's sixty-pound fleece?

Jesus, sometimes I like to wander off and do my own thing. Thank you for always welcoming me back! I love You and want to stay close to You, always.

You can read about your Good Shepherd in Psalm 23.

15

WHAT STINKS?

Create in me a clean heart, O God.

Psalm 51:10

The house smelled like something was burning. Worried, eight-year-old Madelyn followed her nose to the kitchen. Nothing was in the oven. Her investigation led her upstairs, right to her bedroom door. Madelyn peeked inside her room. There, peering back at her with big eyes pleading for help, was Luna, her dog. That "burning" smell now had the distinct odor of . . . a skunk. The poor dog had gone to the corner of Madelyn's house to escape the smell, but she couldn't get away from herself!

We often try to run away from a "stinky problem" too—only to discover the problem is us! Our hearts can give off some seriously funky odors, with scents of jealousy, greed, meanness, and more.

Such "odors" are powerful. Jesus, though, can clean out your heart if you ask him to (Psalm 51:10).

Are you detecting some funky fumes? No matter how stinky your heart attitude, give it to Jesus. He wants you to feel fresh and clean again!

What kinds of funky odors can our hearts give off?

Jesus, You see everything going on inside of me; please clean out my heart, and make me more like You.

You can read King David's prayer for a clean heart in Psalm 51.

16
DON'T GIVE UP

Let's not get tired of doing what is good. . . . We
will reap a harvest of blessing if we don't give up.

Galatians 6:9

When his airplane lost power, Pilot "Sully" Sullenberger had only minutes to save the 150 people on board his plane. Most of us would have panicked. Sully, though, had more than 20,000 hours of flying practice, which amounts to 833 days—or more than 2 years— of training. That's a lot of time in the air! With all that practice, he was able to think quickly and land on New York's Hudson River, rescuing every person on that plane. What a hero!

God is proud when we practice with all our might. We may not save lives like Sully, but each time we practice a sport or an instrument, or do a chore or our homework, God is growing our character: He's helping us get tough! When the time is right, our new superpower strength from practice will "reap a harvest of blessing if we don't give up" (Galatians 6:9).

What do you have to practice today? A sport? Your homework? An art project? Even if your responsibility is boring or tough, stick with it. You'll grow good fruit if you don't give up!

In what ways are you working hard right now? Keep it up!

Jesus, help me practice with all my might. Give me an attitude that doesn't give up—even when life is tough! Thanks for giving me a courageous heart.

You can read about not giving up in James 1:2–4.

17

CLEANING HOUSE

So clean house! Make a clean sweep of malice and pretense, envy, and hurtful talk.

1 Peter 2:1 (MSG)

*H*ave you ever cleaned your room as if you were on a special mission? You didn't just make your bed—you vacuumed. You didn't just dust—you stood on your tippy toes to dust that top shelf. You even sorted through clothes until you had bags full of stuff. And when you finished? You were ready to *drop*—exhausted. In your heart, though, you felt joyously proud of your sparkling clean room.

It felt brand-new.

Just as our rooms need cleaning, our hearts do too. The Bible says: "So clean house! Make a clean sweep of malice and pretense, envy, and hurtful talk" (1 Peter 2:1 MSG).

Bad habits do not disappear right away, even if Jesus lives inside of us. So we need to "clean house," throwing out anything that keeps us from loving God and everyone around us.

Once you do, you'll love the feel of your clean, new space.

Do you have any attitudes or habits that need to be cleaned up today?

Jesus, if there's anything in my heart that needs to be cleaned out, please help me "clean house."

You can read King David's prayer for a clean heart in Psalm 51.

18
FAITH IN ACTION

Pure and genuine religion in the sight of God the Father means caring for orphans.

James 1:27

Katie spent an entire summer break holding babies. Hundreds of tiny, precious babies! The babies at the orphanage where Katie volunteered had food to eat, clothes to wear, and a roof over their heads—but not enough staff to hold them all. Just as much as they need food or shelter, babies need love. That summer, Katie gave them plenty.

By loving on those babies, Katie was putting her faith in action. The Bible says, "Faith by itself isn't enough. Unless it produces good deeds, it is dead and useless" (James 2:17). That means we can't just read the Bible: We have to live it out! We shouldn't only memorize Jesus's words about loving others. We're called to love and serve too!

In fact, we have amazing opportunities to live out our faith right where we are—in our homes, neighborhoods, and schools. Whether that means putting together a Christmas care package for needy kids in our community, or raking the leaves in our neighbor's yard, we can put our faith in action, each and every day.

So, what are you waiting for? Go out and serve!

How can you love and serve your community? Brainstorm some great ideas right now.

Jesus, help me put my faith into action. Show me all the ways I can go out and serve in my home, school, and community this week.

You can read about putting your faith in action in James 2:14–18.

19

THE TURQUOISE MUG

The LORD hears his people when they call to him
for help. He rescues them from all their troubles.
The LORD is close to the brokenhearted; he
rescues those whose spirits are crushed.

Psalm 34:17–18

At summer camp, Hannah created a beautiful clay turquoise mug, one with a lovely golden handle. She couldn't wait to show it off to her parents. Seeing her dad at parent pickup, she began sprinting, mug in hand. Can you guess what happened? In Hannah's excitement, the mug slipped and—crack!—split into two pieces.

That wasn't the end of the turquoise mug, though. Today, it sits on the kitchen counter, on display. If you inspect the mug closely,

though, you'll see its "scar." The place Hannah and her dad glued it back together.

Like Hannah's pieced-together mug, we can accumulate scars too. Scars mark our hurts, the places we've been rejected, overlooked, or disappointed. But they can also tell us a beautiful story: God's love and power to heal us!

Scars aren't something to hide. In fact, they can be the greatest proof of God's healing love and power!

Do you have any scars? What stories do they tell?

Jesus, many things in this world just hurt, and I've picked up a few scars from them too. Thanks for caring for me and for healing even the broken parts of me.

You can read how much God cares for you in Psalm 34:15–20.

20
HONORING OTHERS

Don't look out only for your own interests, but take an interest in others, too.

Philippians 2:4

Do you know the first American to climb Mount Everest? His name is Jim Whittaker, and in 1963, he climbed 29,000 feet—all the way to the top of world's highest mountain. What an amazing accomplishment! Jim didn't do it by himself. His Tibetan guide, Nawang Gombu, helped him every step of the way.

Who should get the honor of reaching the top first? the two had even wondered, when they were a few steps from the summit. Whittaker said Gombu should go first. But Gombu said with a smile, "You first, Big Jim!" They decided to take the final steps together. What a show of humble friendship!

The Bible tells us to honor each other, just as Whittaker and Gombu did. Honoring others could be as small as letting someone go before us in line, or as big as standing up for a friend. Most amazing of all? God gives us all sorts of opportunities to honor those around us—*if* we're searching for them.

So get ready!

Can you think up any exciting ways to honor a friend, family member, or neighbor today?

Jesus, it's fun to think up ways to honor others! Keep my eyes wide open, so that I can see all ways I can help those around me.

You can read how Jesus honored people in Philippians 2:5–11.

21
GIFT-GIVING GOD

If you, then, though you are evil, know how to give good gifts to your children, how much more will your Father in heaven give good gifts to those who ask him!

Matthew 7:11 (NIV)

The two weeks before Christmas, Sophia had secretly inspected each and every gift under the Christmas tree. So when Sophia's mom handed Sophia the gift with the sparkly silver wrapping paper on Christmas morning, she gasped. She recognized the gift, but it wasn't hers. The note, which was no longer there, had been addressed to her mom.

Seeing the excitement in her mother's eyes, she went ahead and opened the gift: a stylish pink blow-dryer, something Sophia had wanted all year!

While struggling to pay the bills, Sophia's mom had still wanted to make Christmas special. So she'd given her own gift to her daughter. But if you'd been there that Christmas morning, you wouldn't have known who gave or received the gift—because both Sophia's and her mom's smiles were so big!

God loves giving us gifts too. In fact, the Bible says your heavenly Father is the best gift-giver: "If you, then, though you are evil, know how to give good gifts to your children, how much more will your Father in heaven give good gifts to those who ask him!" (Matthew 7:9–12 NIV).

Because your heavenly Father is incredibly generous, you can go confidently to Him asking for what you need. He may surprise you with something better than what you could ask for (Ephesians 3:20).

What do you need or want? Talk to your heavenly Father about it.

Jesus, thanks for being the best Gift-Giver. I know that You'll give me what I need for today.

You can read about your gift-giving Father in Matthew 7:7–11.

22

TURTLE TOUGH

We can rejoice, too, when we run into problems and trials, for we know that they help us develop endurance.

Romans 5:3

When baby sea turtles enter our world, they start running. Their first run? A dangerous race across the beach to the ocean (which is a crazy distance with short legs!). And, along the way? Crabs, raccoons—or anything lurking on the beach—is excited to turn them into lunch.

What a scary start, especially for such little dudes! It doesn't seem fair.

Did you know the turtles wouldn't survive the ocean without this journey? Once they reach the sea, they come up against Great White sharks. They face down Orcas. They swim across entire oceans. This first race trains them for the many challenges they will face.

Struggles aren't just for tiny turtles—but for us too! The Bible says, "We can rejoice, too, when we run into problems and trials, for we know that they help us develop endurance" (Romans 5:3). Our challenges can teach us not to give up, helping us become all God is calling us to be.

Are you struggling right now? Maybe your challenge is preparing you for the wild and wonderful adventures God has in store for you.

What kinds of struggles are you facing today?

Jesus, help me not to give up, whatever I face. Give me a brave heart and teach me to become all You're calling me to be.

You can read about not giving up in Hebrews 12:1–3.

23

GOD'S FAVORITE THINGS

Every good and perfect gift is from above, coming down from the Father of the heavenly lights, who does not change like shifting shadows.

James 1:17 (NIV)

*I*magine that in the kitchen, bacon is frying. But there's something really weird: you can't hear the crack-sizzle-pop of the bacon frying up in the pan—or even smell the bacon wafting through the kitchen. It's colorless too. (Yuck.) As you bite into your breakfast, you discover it has no taste. Living in a world like this—a world in which you couldn't use your five senses (your ability to see, smell, hear, taste, or touch)—would be extremely boring, right?

God created our five senses so we could experience all His *favorite things*. Colorful sunsets and sparkling night skies. Soft things that make us go "ooh and aah," from cozy blankets to alpacas (the cutest animals ever). The sweet, refreshing taste of ice cream, the smell of cake baking in the oven. He doesn't want us to miss out on *any* of it.

So, pay attention to the amazing (and sometimes not-so-amazing!) sights, sounds, smells, tastes, and textures all around you. Some of God's favorite things (James 1:17).

≈≈≈≈≈≈

What sense—your ability to see, smell, hear, taste, or touch—would you miss the most if you lost it?

Jesus, thanks for my five senses. Help me use them to pay attention to all the good stuff You've created in the world around me.

You can read how God gave us His favorite things in Genesis 1:26–31.

24
AM I REALLY GROWING?

**Let's not get tired of doing what is good.
At just the right time we will reap a
harvest of blessing if we don't give up.**

Galatians 6:9

Ten-year-old Charlotte and her family had just moved into a
new home. Excitedly, Charlotte started exploring the house.
Just inside her bedroom, she found an abandoned plant—an
orchid that wasn't flowering.

Charlotte placed her new plant into a spot by the window—where
it could get plenty of light. She never forgot to water it. And she
cut off its dead leaves.

But nothing happened.

Week after week, she inspected the plant. No blooms appeared. She
grew discouraged.

"Give it a month," her mom said, "and if nothing has happened by then, maybe just toss it out."

On decision day, Charlotte couldn't believe her eyes. There was a small pink bud.

Sometimes we grow like that orchid. God's work in us is often invisible—at least at first. We aren't always patient with our friends. We may blow up at our siblings. Or we might even make unwise choices. Eventually, God's work in us will break through, for all to see.

How are you growing right now?

Jesus, I don't like being patient; I wish I could grow faster! But even when I can't see it, I know You're growing me, changing me from the inside out.

You can read about growing more like Jesus in 2 Peter 1:5–8.

25

MIRROR, MIRROR

You have searched me, LORD, and you know me. You know when I sit and when I rise; you perceive my thoughts from afar.

Psalm 139:1–2 (NIV)

*I*f you lived hundreds of years ago, you wouldn't have known what you looked like because mirrors weren't around. Until recently, you could only see your reflection in rivers, streams, and puddles. How crazy.

Imagine living without a mirror: you'd go to school wondering if your hair was sticking straight up, your ponytail was messy, or your eyes puffy. Yikes. Before we go out the front door, it's helpful to be able to inspect ourselves.

What if we had a mirror to check out our hearts too? Try it. Before you go to bed each night, put a "mirror" up by asking yourself this question: Do I feel good about my choices today?

Whatever your answer—whether you made some spectacular choices or spectacularly poor ones—talk to God about what you find. Nothing surprises Him. As your Creator, He already knows everything inside your heart and is your biggest fan, no matter what.

{{{{{{

If you had a mirror showing what's going on inside your heart, what would you see right now?

Jesus, You see everything that goes on inside my heart. Even though there's a lot of messiness inside of me, I know You love me just the way that I am.

You can read how God knows everything about you in Psalm 139.

26
LITTLE BY LITTLE

Little by little I will drive them out before you, until you have increased enough to take possession of the land.

Exodus 23:30 (NIV)

*H*ave you ever faced an impossible challenge? Then sit up and listen to this story: After a blizzard, a little girl was supposed to clear a path in front of her house. Her tool to take on the huge snowdrifts? Just a small shovel. When a neighbor saw the small girl shoveling snow piles towering above her head, he laughed.

"How can someone as small as you dig yourself out of snowdrifts this big?" he asked. The girl looked up and replied, "Little by little, that's how!" And she kept on shoveling.

Today you could face something as seemingly impossible as that small girl's. How are you going to finish it? Just tell yourself, "little by little." God led His people into the Promised Land "little by little." He helped them defeat bigger and stronger enemies so they could settle in and make Israel their very own home (Exodus 23:30).

Whatever you're up against today, God wants to encourage you. He'll come alongside you, just as He did for the Israelites. With God's help, you'll rise to the challenge, little by little.

〜〜〜〜〜

What challenging thing do you need to do today "little by little"?

Jesus, sometimes I get anxious thinking about all the things I need to do, but I know You can help me finish them—little by little!

You can read how Israel overcame their enemies "little by little" in Exodus 23:22–30.

27

A FRESH START

Because of the LORD's great love we are not consumed, for his compassions never fail. They are new every morning; great is your faithfulness.

Lamentations 3:22–23 (NIV)

Have you ever read *Anne of Green Gables*? In the classic book, everyone's favorite orphan Anne learns to adjust to life with her new adoptive parents—with hilarious mishaps, mistakes, and many, many adventures along the way!

In one funny part, Anne is baking a cake: by mistake, she adds medicine instead of vanilla. Oh no! Once everyone tries her cake and discovers her big mistake, she says cheerily, "Isn't it nice to think that tomorrow is a new day with no mistakes in it yet?"

How encouraging! We all make mistakes, but tomorrow is a new day—a fresh start. The Bible says, "[God's mercies] are new every morning" (Lamentations 3:23). Even when we mess up, we can always begin again.

What if you've made an unwise choice? Don't beat yourself up about it. Instead, talk to God. Say that you're sorry. He'll forgive you, and tomorrow is a brand-new day, a fresh start!

Where do you need a fresh start? Talk to God about it.

Jesus, thanks for giving me never-ending second chances.

You can read about God's unfailing love in Lamentations 3:22–26.

28

THE KING'S SPECIAL MARK

"I will honor you, Zerubbabel son of Shealtiel, my servant. I will make you like a signet ring on my finger," says the LORD, "for I have chosen you. I, the LORD of Heaven's Armies, have spoken!"

Haggai 2:23

Do you sign your name with big, swirly letters? Or is your handwriting *just right*, with all the letters perfectly inside the lines? However you write it, your signature is unique to you. Your special mark.

In ancient times, the king wouldn't sign his name. Nope. Instead, he would *stamp* his signature using a special ring—a *signet ring*. It had a one-of-a-kind royal symbol: the king's special mark. If you received a letter with this special mark, you knew that it carried the

power of the king—and the entire kingdom—behind it. (It carried lots of *power*!)

In today's Bible reading, God says to the governor Zerubbabel, "I will make you like a signet ring on my finger" (Haggai 2:23). What did God mean? The *King of the universe* (God) had given Zerubbabel His special mark of strength. *Power* to do God's special work. Whoa.

You have God's special mark too! Yes, really. When you follow Him, God gives you His one-of-a-kind special mark—His strength—to do God's amazing work on Earth. You're like God's very own signet ring. (Now, that's a lot of power!)

So be confident today: you've got the special mark of your King.

What does it mean to have God's special mark?

Jesus, how amazing to know that wherever I go and whatever I do, I have Your special mark! Help me to love and obey You so I can do Your special work.

You can read God's message to the governor in Haggai 2:20–23.

29
HOOP PRAYERS

You can pray for anything, and if you believe that you've received it, it will be yours.

Mark 11:24

*A*t youth group, the middle school girls piled on the comfy couches for prayer. Julie opened her mouth to pray but nothing came out! In her heart, she felt nudged to ask for the basketball hoop the youth group wanted.

Does God really answer prayers like that? she thought to herself. Finally, she blurted out, "God, can someone . . . er . . . buy that basketball hoop for us? . . . Yeah, thanks," she finished awkwardly, embarrassed.

That night, the youth group got a call: a family wanted to donate a brand-new basketball hoop for the entire youth group!

As He did for Julie, God loves to show us what to pray. So, quiet yourself and listen. God can put a person, a situation, or even something as random as a basketball hoop on your heart or mind to pray about. Whatever God has placed on your heart, no matter how crazy, pray about it. However God responds—with a "yes," "no," or "not now"—you can be sure that God is listening.

Wait and watch for how God answers!

What situation, person, or thing has God put on your heart to pray for right now?

Jesus, please show me who or what to pray for today. I want to know what's on Your heart and to pray for the things You care about.

You can read how Jesus taught us to pray in Mark 11:22–25.

30

THE CRAZY-EXPENSIVE GIFT

A woman came with an alabaster jar of very
expensive perfume, made of pure nard. She broke
the jar and poured the perfume on his head.

Mark 14:3 (NIV)

In the Bible there's a story about a gift—a crazy-expensive one. A jar of perfume worth more than $20,000—wow! If you had a body spray that expensive, would you put it on every day? No way! Most of us would lock that perfume away, in a very special drawer, wearing it on only the fanciest occasions.

That's what makes the Gift-Giver's action so shocking. In one sitting, the Gift-Giver emptied it. Pouring it out over the One she loved with all her heart.

"What a waste!" cried out everyone in the room, except One.

Jesus—the One who received the gift—knew she was telling Him how much she loved Him. And He loved her, and her gift, with all His heart.

What ways can you show Jesus you love Him? It doesn't matter if you're singing a song, . . . studying for a test, . . . drawing a picture, . . . or helping a brother or sister. Anything and everything can be a gift for Jesus, when given out of a heart of love.

God loves your gifts—and you—with all His heart.

How do you want to show Jesus that you love Him?

Jesus, whatever I do can become a gift for You if it's done in love—and I love You with all my heart.

You can read the Gift-Giver's story in Mark 14:3–9.

31
SMELLS LIKE CHRIST

**Now he uses us to spread the knowledge of
Christ everywhere, like a sweet perfume. Our
lives are a Christ-like fragrance rising up to God.**

2 Corinthians 2:14–15

*D*o you know that you smell amazing? It's true. The Bible says
you have Christ's signature scent—a glorious, life-giving,
full-of-love-and-joy-all-mingled-together, kind of perfume.
The truth is, you can't help but smell like Jesus, because Christ lives
inside of you!

Whenever you walk into a room, others will immediately get a
whiff of your life-giving scent. Followers of Jesus will love your
fragrance. And those curious about Jesus? They'll be crazy about
it too! In fact, God is drawing people into a personal relationship
with Jesus through your winning perfume. Pretty cool, right?

But those who reject God? The Bible says they experience your scent differently. To them, it's a stench. They may even run the other way. And that's OK.

However people experience it, you have a powerful fragrance. You wear the scent of God.

Who do you that know gives off an amazing Christ scent?

Jesus, it's crazy knowing the people around me are drawn to You through my fragrance (which, I guess, is really Your perfume anyway!). I like wearing Your signature scent, and I love You too.

You can read about your Christ scent in 2 Corinthians 2:14–16.

32
GOD'S GALAXIES

**When I look at the night sky and see the work
of your fingers—the moon and the stars you
set in place—what are mere mortals that you
should think about them, human beings that
you should care for them?**

Psalm 8:3–4

On a clear night, imagine stepping outside and looking *up*. The sky is dazzling—stars like jewels light up the night! Gazing at the galaxies, you feel in awe.

On a starlit night just like this, King David looked up too. Amazed, David—a musician as well as a king—wrote this song: "When I look at the night sky and see the work of your fingers—the moon and the stars you set in place—what are mere mortals that you should think about them, human beings that you should care for them?" (Psalm 8:3–4).

When we imagine the cosmic scale of the universe, our problems can seem small. Yet God doesn't think so! Even though God takes care of all the galaxies, He thinks about us too! Not only are we on His mind, but He also cares for us.

King David once wrote that the galaxies and stars shout out just how amazing our God is (Psalm 19:1). Let's join with the stars—and all of creation—in worshiping our awesome God.

Do you like stargazing? Why?

Jesus, when I look up at the stars, I'm amazed by their beauty, and I'm in awe of the size of Your universe too! My problems seem kind of small in comparison, but I know that You care about them too.

You can read about God's amazing creation in Psalm 8:3–9.

33

STOP WORRYING!

**Look at the birds. They don't plant or harvest
or store food in barns, for your heavenly Father
feeds them. And aren't you far more valuable to
him than they are? Can all your worries add a
single moment to your life?**

Matthew 6:26–27

Birds sometimes go to extreme measures to get lunch. But
the bird with the strangest lunch preparation of all? First
prize goes to the Bassian thrush. The bird *farts*—causing
the worms beneath them to wiggle out from under their leaves.
(Probably just to get away from that stinky smell.) And, just like
that, for the little bird, lunch is served! Bizarre, right?

Did you know that Jesus talks about birds and their lunches? He
says, "Look at the birds. They don't plant or harvest or store food

in barns, for your heavenly Father feeds them. And aren't you far more valuable to him than they are? Can all your worries add a single moment to your life?" (Matthew 6:26–27).

Jesus's message to us? Stop worrying! If I've got the birds covered—even the farting Bassian thrush—I've definitely got you too (as you're *way* more important than a bird).

Think about it: Your heavenly Father cared so much about the Bassian thrush that He thought up a crazy—zany—plan just so that they could get lunch. If your heavenly Father went to such great lengths to help out the Bassian thrush, He's not going to forget about you.

He's going to move heaven and earth to solve your problems and to take care of each of your needs. He loves you that much.

꧁꧂

What are you worrying about right now? Talk to God about it.

Jesus, if You can handle feeding each and every bird in the entire world—including ones that fart to find lunch—then taking care of me shouldn't be a problem! Help me to trust in You.

You can read how God cares for every detail of your life in Matthew 6:25–34.

34
HEAVY LIFTING

Give all your worries and cares to God,
for he cares about you.

1 Peter 5:7

*A*lissa found her two-year-old brother, Liam, trying to lift a barbell over his head. What a challenge for a toddler! Even using all his strength, little Liam couldn't pick it up.

Alissa is eight and a strong athlete, so she offered to help. Together they lifted that four-pound weight toward the ceiling. What was so tough for Liam was easy for Alissa!

Just as Liam needed Alissa's help, we need Someone bigger and stronger than we are to carry our problems too. The Bible tells us, "Give all your worries and cares to God, for he cares about you" (1 Peter 5:7). That's an incredible promise, isn't it? Since Jesus is the King of the universe, He has the power to carry our problems in His strong arms.

So, are you tired? Anxious? Lonely? Whatever you're struggling with today, Jesus wants you to hand it over to Him. He can carry your problems—and you too!

&&&&&&&

What worry can you hand over to Jesus right now?

Jesus, You promise that if I give You my worries, You'll carry them. So, here they are. Thanks for loving and caring for me so much that I can run to you whenever I need help or rest.

You can read about giving your problems to God in Matthew 11:28–30.

35

LESSON OF THE HORSE MASK

For [you] are God's masterpiece. He has created [you] anew in Christ Jesus, so [you] can do the good things he planned for [you] long ago.

Ephesians 2:10

*H*ave you ever seen horses wearing masks? To be honest, they look a little silly wearing them. You may even wonder how they can see with a mask covering their eyes. Made of mesh, the masks actually allow horses to see straight through them—while keeping flies out. And it's the flies that spread nasty eye diseases to horses. That's why the masks don't blind the horses; they protect them from going blind!

We could think something similar about the Bible as could be assumed about those masks. The Bible's guidance can seem like it keeps us from seeing, and joining in on, all the fun! But it's the opposite. Just like those masks protect horses from going blind, the Bible's wisdom keeps us from being infected by lies that make us blind to good things—especially God's amazing plans for us.

The Bible tells us, "For we are God's masterpiece. He has created us anew in Christ Jesus, so we can do the good things he planned for us long ago" (Ephesians 2:10). Through the Bible and prayer, God opens our eyes to what life is really about!

How does God's Word open our eyes to what life is really about?

Jesus, thanks for the Bible: I love your Word! Through it, You share Your exciting plans and purposes for me. What a treasure.

You can read about God's plans for you in Ephesians 2:8–10.

36
THE ROCK

You are Peter (which means "rock"), and upon
this rock I will build my church.

Matthew 16:18

Have you ever gone climbing on huge boulders? If you have,
then you know they're close to unmovable. No matter how
hard you try to push them, they won't budge.

Jesus named one of His disciples "the Rock" (*Peter* in Greek),
because one day God would build His church on the unbudging
strength Peter found in God. First Peter needed to grow into his
name. Peter was all big talk—even bragging he'd die for Jesus—but
he couldn't keep his promises.

On the night Jesus needed him most, Peter ran.

On his own, Peter discovered he wasn't like a rock. But when God filled him with the Holy Spirit's power at Pentecost, Peter changed. He lived up to his name, even risking his life for Christ.

Ask the Holy Spirit to fill you up with His life and power today! As He did for Peter, Jesus wants to give you a brave heart.

How did Peter grow into his name?

Jesus, I'm imperfect, just like Peter. I really need Your power to do the right thing. Please fill me up with Your Holy Spirit and give me Your amazing power and strength today.

You can read Peter's story in Acts 3:1–10.

37

THE ROARING LION

Stay alert! Watch out for your great enemy, the devil. He prowls around like a roaring lion, looking for someone to devour. Stand firm against him, and be strong in your faith.

1 Peter 5:8–9

The last time you visited the zoo, what were the lions up to? Likely, they were taking their catnaps (they like their beauty sleep—just like us). In the wild, lions can't sleep all the time if they want to survive. They have to hunt. And what stealthy hunters they are: when they see a zebra or antelope or gazelle, they crouch in the tall grass, creep forward, and—*pounce*—they attack.

The Bible tells us that Satan—the devil—is like "a roaring lion" (1 Peter 5:8). A sneaky hunter, he attacks us when we're already

tired or scared or lonely, whenever we're vulnerable. Here's some good news: one day King Jesus will defeat him for good.

Until that day, be on your guard against your Enemy and his lies. But don't be afraid. If you're ever attacked, just say, "In Jesus's name, go away." The devil will scram (James 4:7). The devil is a predator, yes. But here's the thing, he's no match for your Savior. With Jesus alive inside of you, you are protected from the roaring lion.

Have you ever seen a lion at the zoo? What were they up to?

Jesus, I don't have to be afraid of the roaring lion—Satan— because You live inside of me, and he's no match for You! Thanks for protecting me against my Enemy.

You can learn how to fight the Enemy in James 4:7–8.

38

BODY TALK

The human body has many parts, but the many parts make up one whole body. So it is with the body of Christ.

1 Corinthians 12:12

Did you know that your liver has a superpower? If it's damaged or cut, this incredible organ grows back. Gross (and kind of cool), right? Now, likely, you didn't wake up this morning thinking about your liver, but daily it cleans out poisons from your body. Your body depends on your liver—along with all your other organs—to survive.

The Bible compares the human body to the church. As your human body has different parts—each working together to keep you in great shape—your church needs each person in it to make it healthy too.

So, you may be asking, What does this mean for me? Just this: your church can't run without *you*. Your church needs your voice and your gifts to be healthy and strong.

Are you involved at your church? If you are, how?

Jesus, show me how I can use my gifts to make a difference in my church.

You can read how your church needs your voice in 1 Corinthians 12:12–27.

39

WORST HOMEWORK ASSIGNMENT EVER

The LORD would speak to Moses face to face, as one speaks to a friend.

Exodus 33:11 (NIV)

What would you do if you had a homework assignment that lasted more than a year? How about ten years? Forty years? If homework assignments were ranked, surely this would be the worst homework assignment ever.

In the Old Testament, God gave Moses a homework assignment just like that. His task? To guide grumpy people for more than forty years in a blazing hot desert, leading them home to God's Promised Land. That's a long time! In a hot desert. With grumpy people.

(Poor Moses.)

Moses was able to do the impossible because "the LORD would speak to Moses face to face, as one speaks to a friend" (Exodus 33:11 NIV). Through God's friendship, Moses completed his homework assignment and got those grumpy people home.

Each day, God has homework for us. Sometimes our assignments appear small. Maybe yours is being kind to your brother or sister. If your sibling, though, is anything like the Israelites—a bit grumpy—then you have a big assignment disguised as a small one. Whatever the size of your task, you need God's help to finish it.

Spend time talking with your heavenly Father, as Moses did. Through His power alive in you, you'll do the seemingly impossible too.

What is something that seems impossible for you today? Ask God for help.

Jesus, some of Your homework assignments seem impossible (including loving my family), but You'll help me do all things through Your incredible strength.

You can read about Moses's crazy homework assignment in Exodus 3:1–8.

40
PAINFUL PRUNING

My Father is the gardener. He cuts off every branch of mine that doesn't produce fruit, and he prunes the branches that do bear fruit so they will produce even more.

John 15:1–2

Jenna loved her grandmother's rose garden. All summer long, she watched the wild and sweet-smelling roses bloom.

Then came the first frost. It was time to lop off the roses and prune the branches. Why? As strange as it sounds, pruning roses is the only way for them to grow even more blooms the next year.

Just as pruning makes way for growth in roses, sometimes God needs to do some pruning in us. He is a good Gardener: "he prunes the branches that do bear fruit so they will produce even more" (John 15:1–2). He wants us to be fruitful!

Pruning can be uncomfortable, and sometimes it really hurts. God isn't out to hurt us—but He can take any tough situation in our lives and use it for good. Everything, even the toughest stuff, can help us become more like our Savior, Jesus.

If you're going through a hard time, have hope! God is growing something exquisitely beautiful inside of you. One day, you'll see all that good fruit.

How does God prune our hearts?

Jesus, I don't like going through tough things. No one does. But You can take even the toughest stuff in my life and use it for good. Thanks for growing beautiful things in me.

You can read about your Gardener in John 15:1–5.

41

THREE FEARLESS FRIENDS

We will never serve your gods or worship the
gold statue you have set up.

Daniel 3:18

Meet three best friends from the Bible—Shadrach, Meshach, and Abednego. (Try repeating all of their names three times fast—quite a tongue twister!)

Their story began when King Nebuchadnezzar ordered everyone to bow to a gold statue—of himself. The statue was enormous: ninety feet high and nine feet wide. (Nebuchadnezzar was full of himself!) Shadrach, Meshach, and Abednego had a challenging choice: would they follow God, or would they do what everyone else was doing?

Have you ever faced a decision like that?

In this story, the three friends bravely remained standing—even when everyone else kneeled down. Furious, the king gave them one last chance to bow, or they would be burned alive.

"If you throw us in the fire, the God we serve can rescue us," they told the king, "but even if he doesn't, . . . we still wouldn't serve your gods or worship the gold statue you set up" (Daniel 3:17–18 MSG).

Shadrach, Meshach, and Abednego were willing to die rather than disobey God. How courageous!

While God did miraculously rescue them (be sure to read the story in your Bible!), the friends showed fearless faith.

✂✂✂✂✂

How do you need to be brave right now?

Jesus, give me courage to make wise choices even when I am afraid or friends disagree with my decisions.

You can read the story of these three fearless friends in Daniel 3:1–30.

42

GOOD MORNING, MIGHTY HERO

Then the angel of the LORD came and sat beneath the great tree at Ophrah, which belonged to Joash of the clan of Abiezer. Gideon son of Joash was threshing wheat at the bottom of a winepress to hide the grain from the Midianites. The angel of the LORD appeared to him and said, "Mighty hero, the LORD is with you!"

Judges 6:11–12

There once was a young guy who was very frightened. He was so afraid, in fact, that when we meet him in the book of Judges, Gideon is hiding away, in a wine press.

"Mighty hero, the LORD is with you!" an angel greeted him. God had specially chosen Gideon to conquer Israel's enemy, the angel said.

Gideon—hiding out and afraid—a mighty warrior? you may be asking. Seems kind of like a joke. Even Gideon thought the angel had the wrong guy. But God promised to be with Gideon and to make him successful in his fight against Israel's enemies. Believing God's promises, Gideon brought Israel victory.

God chooses ordinary people like Gideon—like us—for His plans. We may or may not be the bravest or the strongest or the most popular. But here's the thing: we have God on our side. And you know that with God's help, we can do all things.

Do you have a seemingly impossible task? No matter what it is, God promises to help. Hear Him whisper to you, "Mighty hero, I am with you!"

ﾞﾞﾞﾞﾞ

Why do you think God chose someone like Gideon?

Jesus, no matter the size of the assignment or how difficult the situation, I can do all things in Your amazing power. Like Gideon, help me trust and believe You when You promise to fight for me.

You can read Gideon's story in Judges 6:11–16.

43

FACING YOUR FEARS

In this world you will have trouble. But take heart! I have overcome the world.

John 16:33 (NIV)

*H*as something ever been too big or scary for you to face? Maybe it was starting a new school year? Or trying out for the class play? Or taking your science test? Or even making new friends? These moments can make us afraid or anxious!

Because God is bigger than any problem or situation we could ever face, we can run to Him and receive the courage to face our fears. All you have to do is tell Jesus you're scared. And then ask Him for help. Jesus tells us, "In this world you will have trouble. But take heart! I have overcome the world" (John 16:33 NIV).

Jesus is always ready and available to help us! In fact, helping out His kids is one of His favorite things to do. So, just ask.

What's something too big for you to face right now? Take time to talk to Jesus about it. He'll help you!

Jesus, because You're bigger than anything I fear, please give me the courage to face each situation that comes my way today.

You can read about talking to God in Philippians 4:6–7.

44

NEVER ALONE

**Be sure of this: I am with you always,
even to the end of the age.**

Matthew 28:20

Colombian soccer player Radamel Falcao scored in the seventieth minute of the 2018 World Cup game—helping his team beat Poland. It wasn't just a win for the team. The goal—his thirtieth—was also a win for Falcao. Falcao had now scored more goals than any other Colombian player, ever. Simply put, Falcao is the best of the best.

Falcao loves Jesus too. His fans know it. How? Whenever he lifts up his jersey, they see a shirt that says, *Con Jesus nunca estara solo*: "With Jesus you'll never be alone."

This message points to a promise Jesus gave to His disciples: "I am with you always, even to the end of the age" (Matthew 28:20). He wanted to encourage them, that although he was returning to heaven, He'd send His own Spirit—the Holy Spirit—to them. He'd live forever inside them!

Christ gives us the same promise: No matter where we go, whether close to home or faraway, we can receive the amazing joy and comfort knowing He's with us.

How does the promise that Jesus is always with you provide you encouragement?

Jesus, thank You that I'm never alone because You're with me.

You can read Jesus's promise to always be with you in Matthew 28:16–20.

45

CHOROPOLY

God told them, "I've never quit loving you and never will. Expect love, love, and more love!

Jeremiah 31:3 (MSG)

*E*very Saturday night, the Johnson family comes together to play Monopoly. But their version is called *Choropoly*. That's because the kids can earn Monopoly money throughout the week by doing chores. If they make their beds or wash the dishes, they can collect more money—helping them buy more properties during the Monopoly game. But if they forget to do their chores? They lose that money, and, often, their chance to win. For the Johnsons, it literally *pays* to do chores!

Getting paid in Monopoly money makes chores more fun. But we can breathe a sigh of relief that God's love doesn't work like that. Think about it: We can't earn—or lose—God's love. Ever. God doesn't love you more when you make your bed, . . . get perfect grades, . . . perform your piano solo perfectly, . . . or are very good. He also doesn't love you any less if your room is a mess, . . . you lie, . . . or you fail all your tests.

God's love is a free gift. All you have to do is accept it.

Do you have to perform to get God's love? Why or why not?

Jesus, help me remember that no matter what I do, Your love for me doesn't change. Thanks for loving me just the way that I am.

You can read about God's crazy love for you in John 3:16–17.

46
BEST FRIENDS

No power in the sky above or in the earth below—indeed, nothing in all creation will ever be able to separate us from the love of God that is revealed in Christ Jesus our Lord.

Romans 8:39

Who do you want to be your best friend? Probably someone who is always there for you (and someone you can have fun with too!).

Best friends David and Jonathan were always there for each other, even when it wasn't easy. You probably know David—the brave teen who killed Goliath with a sling and a stone and who later became king. His friend Jonathan was a prince, the crown prince in fact, which means Jonathan—not David—was supposed to be king.

Was Jonathan jealous when God chose his best friend to be king instead? No way! Rather, Jonathan promised David they'd be friends forever—and he stuck to his promise (1 Samuel 20), even hiding and protecting David from King Saul when the king tried to hurt his friend (you can read more about their true friendship in today's Bible reading).

Real friends like David and Jonathan give us a tiny picture of God's never-let-you-down, always-on-your-side friendship. The Bible says nothing—absolutely nothing—can separate us from His love (Romans 8:38–39). He's always watching over us.

What do you like about David and Jonathan's friendship?

Jesus, thanks for being the God of the universe—and my Friend. Help me remember that You're always there for me—that You're always on my side!

You can read David and Jonathan's story in 1 Samuel 18:1–4.

47
NOT FEAR BUT FAITH

They said, "We scouted out the land from one end to the other—it's a land that swallows people whole. Everybody we saw was huge. . . . Alongside them we felt like grasshoppers. And they looked down on us as if we were grasshoppers."

Numbers 13:32–33 (MSG)

*H*ave you ever been asked to step out and be brave? Maybe you were asked to speak in front of your class? Or join a new sports team? Or take an art class?

God asked the Israelites to step out and be brave too, to move into His Promised Land. When He sent spies to check it out, though, all but two spies freaked out.

"Giants were in the land!" they reported. "Next to them we're like grasshoppers," they said.

The two brave spies Caleb and Joshua stood up. They challenged everyone: "You've forgotten the most important thing—God is on our side!"

But no one listened to them. Because of fear, the Israelites walked around a desert for forty years before entering the Promised Land. It's a sad story, really.

Sometimes our fear controls us, just as it did for the Israelites. If that happens to you, you can stop and ask God for help, even a simple "Help me, God!" will do. He'll listen to you. Remember He's promised to walk beside you, go before you, and be with you.

So what are you waiting for? Go out and try something new! God's got you.

꧁꧂

What's something new that you'd like to try out? Go for it!

Jesus, sometimes my fears shake up my faith. But I don't need to be afraid, because wherever I go and whatever I do, You're with me. Help me to be brave and try new things!

You can read the Israelites' story in Numbers 13:25–14:9.

48
FEEDING OURSELVES

Anyone who lives on milk is still a baby. That person does not want to learn about living a godly life. Solid food is for those who are grown up. They have trained themselves to tell the difference between good and evil. That shows they have grown up.

Hebrews 5:13–14 (NIrV)

Captured on the webcam, the baby eagles—eaglets—were hungry. Mom and Dad, though, weren't paying attention. Just behind the eaglets lay a big fish. Even though it could feed all three eaglets, they couldn't feed themselves. Soon, their parents would teach them—one of their first survival lessons.

We're like those eaglets when we first begin a relationship with God. We need to be fed spiritually, by our parents or maybe our pastors or other trusted adults. As we mature, though, we get to feed ourselves.

In fact, God has been joyously preparing for this day, when you'd be old enough to spend time together—just the two of you. Think of it as a special date with your King. So, claim your most comfortable chair. Wear your coziest pj's. And bring your journal, in preparation to talk with God. Or find the biggest space in your house and turn up the music—for a dance party!

Whether you're dancing and singing praises to Jesus, or quietly journaling your prayers, Jesus is waiting, just for you.

What are some fun ways to spend time with Jesus? Journaling? Reading the Bible? Worshiping and having a dance party? Brainstorm some fun ideas now.

Jesus, You're amazing, and I can't wait to get to know You better. Show me some fun ways that we can spend time together.

You can read about spiritual food in Hebrews 5:12–6:2.

49
WRONG TURN?

Then Jonah prayed to the Lord his God from inside the fish. He said, "I cried out to the Lord in my great trouble, and he answered me."

Jonah 2:1–2

Have you ever taken a wrong turn? A runner in a half marathon missed her turn, accidently running twenty-six miles—a whole marathon! Not only did she run thirteen extra miles, but she also ran it *fast*. Fast enough, in fact, to qualify for one of the most famous marathons in the world, the Boston Marathon. Pretty cool, right?

In the Bible, there's a story about a prophet who took a wrong turn, but his was on purpose. When God told Jonah to go to the city of Nineveh, Jonah hopped onto a boat heading the opposite direction.

Amazingly, Jonah thought he could run away from God (considering God sees and knows everything, you may think his plan a bit silly!). When his plan landed him in the belly of a fish, Jonah gave up running. He cried out for help, and God rescued Him.

God hears us, too, when we cry out to Him after we've been on the run. If you've gone the wrong way through an unwise choice, stop. Ask for God's forgiveness. He'll get you back on the right track.

⸎⸎⸎⸎⸎⸎

Have you ever taken a wrong turn when traveling? How long did it take to find the right path?

Jesus, You see everything I do. Whenever I make a poor choice—and take a wrong turn—help me find the right path again.

You can read Jonah's story in Jonah 1:1–2:2.

50
LITTLE BABIES

For you created my inmost being;
you knit me together in my mother's womb.

Psalm 139:13 *(NIV)*

What is it about babies that makes us smile? Maybe they make us smile because we're in awe of a new life—so precious, tiny, and full of promise. Seeing a baby can help us remember our awesome God who loves us so much He gave us life. "For you created my inmost being," the psalmist said. "You knit me together in my mother's womb" (Psalm 139:13 NIV).

Not only does God give us physical life, but, when we begin a relationship with Jesus, we are reborn! We're like newborn babies, spiritually. God also promises that we will live forever and even receive new and better bodies when Jesus comes back!

Life now and forever is definitely something to celebrate!

What's it like knowing God knew you before you were even born?

Jesus, babies are so amazing! Thank You for the gift of life, and the joy of living forever with You too!

You can read about how God specially created you in Psalm 139:13–16.

51

TOGETHER IS BETTER!

Two people are better off than one, for they can help each other succeed. If one person falls, the other can reach out and help.

Ecclesiastes 4:9

Sian Welch and Wendy Ingraham were all-stars. They were competing in the Ironman Triathlon, a one hundred forty mile race of swimming, biking, and running that only the toughest and bravest athletes ever dare try! And not only were they competing in it; they were about to finish strong.

In fact, the finish line was in view.

Exhausted, the runners persevered on wobbly legs, until Welch bumped into Ingraham. Each dropped to the ground. Struggling to stand up, they fell again—just a few feet from the finish line. But

these two champion athletes weren't giving up. No way! Ingraham began crawling, so did Welch. The crowd roared as Ingraham crossed the finish line in fourth place, everyone surrounding her to give her hugs.

Instead of staying to enjoy their praise, she did something unexpected. She turned around, reaching out her hand to her competitor. Welch lunged forward, grabbing Ingraham's outstretched hand. Together, they crossed the finish line. And the crowd went wild!

Sometimes we need help to finish strong (Ecclesiastes 4:9). That's normal. At one time or another, we all fall, whether physically or emotionally. It's amazing to know we're not alone as we press in. Just as our loving Father helps us, we can help others too! By reaching out to them, we can let them know they're not alone.

How can you encourage someone this week?

Jesus, thank You for always being with me. Help me reach out to others too, letting them know they're not alone.

You can read about the power of friendship in Ecclesiastes 4:9–11.

52

ONE HUNDRED YEARS TO GROW UP

He who began a good work in you will carry it on to completion until the day of Christ Jesus.

Philippians 1:6 (NIV)

Of all reptiles, mammals, amphibians, and birds, which species lives the longest? The winner is the mysterious Greenland shark, which makes its home in the icy Arctic. Some of these big sharks are more than five hundred years old! They grow up slowly too. At age fifty, they're still kids. At one hundred? They're teens. Only by age one hundred fifty are the sharks all grown-up. (Imagine waiting over one hundred years to move out of your parents' house!)

Sometimes it seems as if we grow as slowly as a Greenland shark, especially when it comes to heart stuff. We find ourselves making lots of mistakes: We blow up at our siblings or parents. We aren't patient. And we often have an attitude.

The Bible encourages us that, even if we can't see it, God is working on our hearts: "He who began a good work in you will carry it on to completion" (Philippians 1:6 NIV). Did you catch that? God promises to complete all the good stuff He started in you.

But the growth that happens in our hearts takes time. Here's the good news: you'll grow up *way* faster than a Greenland shark.

✿✿✿✿✿✿

Can you imagine being a kid for more than one hundred years?

Jesus, thanks for never giving up on me—for loving me no matter what I do. Help me grow more and more like You.

You can read about spiritual growth in Philippians 1:3–6.

53

CRASH!

On the seventh day God had finished his work of creation, so he rested from all his work. And God blessed the seventh day and declared it holy, because it was the day when he rested from all his work of creation.

Genesis 2:2–3

*I*sla brought home Bailey, her brand-new German Shepherd puppy. Excited about her new home, the puppy ran endlessly around Isla's backyard. After a few hours of this, you can imagine what happened to Bailey: plopping down at her owner's feet, the puppy fell fast asleep.

Have you ever crashed like Bailey? You've been on the go: driving to and from school, sports practice, and various activities, and, suddenly—kerplunk!—you're out, off dreaming.

God created you to rest. Rest matters so much to Him, in fact, that He even dedicated a whole day of the week just for rest. After God created the world and everything in it, God himself took a break on the seventh day, calling it the Sabbath. (If the God of the universe wanted a break, can you imagine how much more you would need one?)

Rest is a gift from our Creator, who knows exactly what we need. So, if you've been on the go, go, go, be like Bailey—and crash!

※※※※※

Have you ever had to stop and crash?

Jesus, sometimes I get so busy I forget to rest. Help me rest when I need it and be all that You created me to be.

You can read about rest in Psalm 23.

54

WARRIOR POWER

It is better to be patient than to fight. It is better to control your temper than to take a city.

Proverbs 16:32 (NIrV)

*H*ave you ever been ready to explode in anger? Maybe your sister visited your closet and put on your favorite shirt . . . without asking. In that moment, you started to boil. Your heart began to race. And your face turned beet red.

Right then, would it be wise to explain to your sister that borrowing your shirt without asking wasn't very considerate?

Probably not (at least if you wanted her to listen to you!).

It's easy to explode in anger. When that happens, though, we often say or do things we later regret. The Bible tells us that controlling our temper makes us even stronger than a warrior (Proverbs 16:32). Self-control makes us *powerful*!

The next time you see your sister wearing your favorite shirt without asking, remember that you have power! First, take a deep breath. Maybe count to ten. Or walk away to cool down a few minutes (or an hour or two). Once your face has returned to its normal shade, humbly share with your sister how her actions made you feel.

In that moment, you're a girl of real power—stronger than even the mightiest warrior.

In what ways can you be powerful when you're angry (for example, take a deep breath and hold it, or count to ten)?

Jesus, when I'm angry, it's easy to blow up. Please give me the strength to have self-control; make me mightier than a warrior.

You can read about self-control in Proverbs 15:18.

55

NOT MY WORRY

**Give your burdens to the LORD, and he
will take care of you.**

Psalm 55:22

Do you ever worry? Well, maybe you can relate to the man who worried about *everything*. One day, everything changed for him. His friends noticed he was relaxed, making jokes, even whistling! "What happened?" his friends asked him, amazed.

He said, "I'm paying someone else to do my worrying for me."

"How much do you pay him?" they asked.

"Two thousand dollars a week," he replied.

"Wow! How can you afford that?"

"I can't," he said, "but that's his worry."

Need someone to give your worries to?

The Bible tells us God wants to carry our worries: "Give your burdens to the Lord, and he will take care of you" (Psalm 55:22). As someone who hung each star in the sky, He has the power and wisdom to hold even our biggest problem.

So, instead of worrying, plop that burden right down on God. The Creator of the world can hold you—and all your problems—safely in His strong arms!

What worry do you want to give to God? Imagine you're handing it over to Him—how does that feel?

Jesus, I worry a lot. There seems to be a lot to worry about! So, right now, in this very moment, I give my worries to You. Thanks for carrying them, so I don't have to.

You can read about God's strength in Isaiah 40:25–31.

56

WAITING IS TOUGH!

**God remembered Noah and all the wild animals
and livestock with him in the boat.**

Genesis 8:1

Imagine your teacher just announced that you're taking a field trip. Maybe it's to a big city or your favorite aquarium or zoo. You can't wait to travel on a bus with your friends to start your adventure. But it's still a month away. That feels like forever.

Waiting is not easy.

In the Bible story of Noah's ark, Noah and his family were stuck on the ark for more than a year. That is a long time on a ship. Especially with smelly animals (and stinky people too).

Maybe during that year, they asked, "Has God forgotten about us? Are we lost out here?"

But God cared for them so much that He wanted everything to be just right when they left the ark.

First God sent a mighty wind to push back the water. Then the ark rested on a mountain. Soon after, Noah sent out a dove, and it didn't come back, because it had found dry land.

Finally, God said it was time to leave the ark. God knew what He was doing. Sometimes God calls us to wait.

Waiting is tough! When have you had to wait for something?

Jesus, waiting isn't easy for me. When I'm waiting for something, please help me to be patient!

You can read Noah's story in Genesis 8:1–12.

57

PEOPLE POWER

He makes the whole body fit together perfectly.
As each part does its own special work, it helps
the other parts grow, so that the whole body is
healthy and growing and full of love.

Ephesians 4:16

*I*n Australia, a man was boarding a train when he slipped—and his leg got stuck in the space between the platform and the train! Coming together, the other passengers pushed the train away from the platform. The trapped man was freed! Now that's people power.

People power is God's plan for building up His family too. In the church, everybody has a job to do. We're each given spiritual gifts—gifts like teaching, truth-telling, encouraging, and more—to cheer on God's family. (Check out the many different spiritual gifts in today's Bible reading!) No one in God's family can sit on the sidelines, just watching the action. We need each other.

Ask Jesus to show you your special job in encouraging God's family.

llllll

What spiritual gifts has God given you?

Jesus, thanks for giving each of us a big role in building up Your family. Show me the gifts You've given me to build up— and cheer on—Your family.

You can read about God's amazing gifts in Romans 12:4–8.

58

ALL THE FEELS

Jesus wept.

John 11:35 (NIV)

*H*ave you ever been so crushed one moment that you burst into tears—only to laugh out loud the next because you so felt full of joy? Our emotions can be confusing!

Jesus felt the same crazy ups and downs—He was indescribably joyful when playing with kids. But, with people who were cheating the helpless? He got angry. In today's Bible story (John 11:32–44), Jesus even cries! Just as we would be, He's heartbroken because His friend, Lazarus, died.

If you're experiencing a roller coaster of emotions, know Jesus has been there. Living inside of you, He even feels each of your feelings

with you. Seriously. Are you having an amazing day? Your Savior rejoices with you. Have you been rejected or excluded? Your Savior cries for you, heartbroken too.

You have emotions, in fact, because you're created in God's image. And God has all the feels.

ﾞﾞﾞﾞﾞﾞ

What are you feeling today? Talk to Jesus about your feelings—and hear what He has to say about them.

Jesus, my emotions sometimes take me on a roller-coaster ride; they make me go crazy. Thanks for knowing what that feels like—for knowing me better than I know myself.

You can read how Jesus experienced big emotions: heartbreak (John 11:32–44); anger (John 2:13–17); joy (Luke 10:21; John 15:11); loneliness (Isaiah 53:3); compassion (Matthew 15:29–39).

59

GREATEST GIFT

For this is how God loved the world: He gave his one and only Son, so that everyone who believes in him will not perish but have eternal life. God sent his Son into the world not to judge the world, but to save the world through him.

John 3:16–17

She should've gotten a ticket. When the police officer stopped her, the mom had been driving with her daughter, who wasn't in a car seat. The law called for the car seat. But the mom had been struggling to make ends meet—and couldn't afford one. Instead of fining them, the officer told the mom and daughter to meet him at the nearby mall. There, he bought them the needed car seat. What an amazing example of generosity.

God's generosity is like that to us, only on a much bigger scale! Our sins—when we act, think, and do things that go against God's best for us—make us guilty too. The Bible says, "But God showed his great love for us by sending Christ to die for us while we were still sinners" (Romans 5:8). God loved us so much that He sent Jesus to Earth to give us the incredible gift of grace, wiping out our guilt from sin for all time! Not only that, but through His actions, Jesus made us "friends of God" (v. 11).

Now that's truly the greatest gift.

How can you be generous toward someone today?

Jesus, thank You for loving me so much that You sacrificed Your life on a cross to free me from my sins. Now that's the best gift ever!

You can read about God's gift of grace in Ephesians 1:1–10.

60

FRIENDSHIP POWER

When Moses' hands grew tired, they took a
stone and put it under him and he sat on it.
Aaron and Hur held his hands up—one on
one side, one on the other—so that his hands
remained steady till sunset.

Exodus 17:12 (NIV)

For her fifth-grade graduation, Twila nervously stepped up to
the podium. When the principal handed her the microphone,
Twila was so full of nerves that she couldn't even face the
audience. So she turned around. The crowd whispered words of encouragement. She didn't budge. Finally, a friend came to the rescue:
leaving her own seat, she stood beside Twila. With the principal
on one side of Twila and her friend on the other, the three read her
speech together. What an amazing show of support!

Moses needed his friends too. In one of Israel's battles, Moses's job was to raise his staff high. If that sounds silly to you, here's the thing: whenever Moses raised his staff, the Israelites took down their enemies. And when he lowered it? The Israelites started losing (Exodus 17:11). Hours into the battle, Moses grew tired.

His buddies came to the rescue: "Aaron and Hur held his hands up—one on one side, one on the other—so that his hands remained steady till sunset" (Exodus 17:12 NIV). Wow! With their support, Moses never gave up. The Israelites won the fight.

Maybe someone needs your encouragement today, just as Moses needed Aaron and Hur. Keep your eyes wide open for how you can help a friend.

Who needs your encouragement today?

Jesus, keep my eyes wide open to see the needs of the people around me. Show me who needs some encouragement today.

You can read Moses's battle story in Exodus 17:8–16.

61

AMAZING LANGUAGES

Suddenly, there was a sound from heaven like the roaring of a mighty windstorm, and it filled the house where they were sitting. Then, what looked like flames or tongues of fire appeared and settled on each of them. And everyone present was filled with the Holy Spirit and began speaking in other languages, as the Holy Spirit gave them this ability.

Acts 2:2–4

*H*ave you ever been to a place—maybe a big city—where you could hear conversations in different languages? It's pretty awesome.

If you had been in Jerusalem on the day Pentecost, you would have heard people speaking in many languages too, as families

from every corner of the world came for the spring harvest celebration! Then, something miraculous happened. When the Holy Spirit came down in "flames or tongues of fire," resting on Jesus's followers, suddenly the disciples could speak the languages of all the city's visitors (Acts 2:3–4). How amazing! Because they heard Jesus's story in their own language, three thousand of them started a relationship with Jesus that day.

We may not speak many languages, but the Holy Spirit helps us connect with people in other ways. Amazingly, we are God's hands and feet—and mouth—to live out His purpose in the world. Today, how can you—with the Holy Spirit's help—reach out to someone unlike you?

What part of today's Bible story amazes you? Why?

Jesus, show me how to reach out to someone who is unlike me today. Thanks for teaching me how to love others through Your Holy Spirit.

You can read the miraculous story of Pentecost in Acts 2:1–12.

62
GENTLE AND STRONG

He got up, rebuked the wind and said to the
waves, "Quiet! Be still!" Then the wind died
down and it was completely calm.

Mark 4:39 (NIV)

*J*ackson is a strong dog—large, tough, and weighing one hundred pounds! Yet even the smallest people love him.

Once, a four-year-old girl spotted Jackson across a room. At first, she was afraid. Then she shyly walked up to him and spent several minutes talking to him and petting him. She discovered he's both gentle and powerful.

This special set of qualities—being gentle and strong—is something we find in Jesus. Little children loved Jesus: they would run up to Him, sit on His lap, and tell Him their secrets. At the same time, Jesus had real power. At His command, demons fled. Huge storms disappeared. And dead people came back to life! Wow.

If we focus only on Jesus's power, we might see him as a superhero—Someone incredibly strong but distant (it's hard to get to know a superhero!). Yet if we think of Him as only gentle, we might forget that Jesus is the Creator of the universe, who hung each star in the sky, placed each planet in orbit, and who made each of us.

The truth is Jesus is *both* of these amazing qualities. He's strong enough for you to trust Him with your whole heart, yet humble enough to call you friend.

ﻼﻼﻼﻼﻼ

When you think of Jesus, do you imagine Him being gentle or powerful or both?

Jesus, You're amazing—thanks for being strong and gentle! Because You're mighty, I know I can always run to You whenever I need help.

You can read about Jesus's gentleness in Matthew 19:13–15 and His power in Mark 4:35–41.

63

A WISE HEART

That night the LORD appeared to Solomon in a dream, and God said, "What do you want? Ask, and I will give it to you!"

1 Kings 3:5

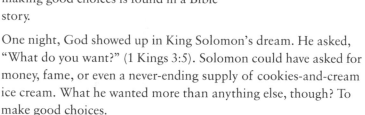

Did you know that you make over three thousand choices each day? Crazy, right? That number only grows as you get older—up to thirty-five thousand choices daily. The secret to making good choices is found in a Bible story.

One night, God showed up in King Solomon's dream. He asked, "What do you want?" (1 Kings 3:5). Solomon could have asked for money, fame, or even a never-ending supply of cookies-and-cream ice cream. What he wanted more than anything else, though? To make good choices.

God gave Solomon just what he asked for—a wise heart. (He even threw in a few extras, like riches and fame too. Solomon became so rich, in fact, that silver became worthless in his kingdom because gold was everywhere!) From this time until today, Solomon became famous, all over the world, for making good choices.

Today you've got three thousand choices ahead of you. Like Solomon, ask God for wisdom. If you ask, God promises to give you a wise heart.

What's a wise choice you've made?

Jesus, I've got so many choices to make today. Please help me make good ones—give me a wise heart.

You can read King Solomon's story in 1 Kings 3:5–15.

64
HEART TO SERVE

A new command I give you: Love one another. As I have loved you, so you must love one another.

John 13:34 (NIV)

When Katie Davis Majors met her neighbor Agnes—a nine-year-old orphan with a big smile—she had no idea Agnes would one day call her "Mommy."

At nineteen, Katie moved to Uganda to serve God and kids. She began teaching at a kindergarten in a small village, where she met Agnes, who lived in a mud hut near Katie's home.

One day, during a heavy rainstorm, the roof of Agnes's hut collapsed, with Agnes inside.

Katie rushed Agnes to the hospital and, later, invited her stay with her. Today Katie is adoptive mom to Agnes—and twelve other girls who were orphaned or neglected. Following Jesus has led Katie to love kids in big ways.

Whether you go to a faraway place like Uganda or serve in your own neighborhood, Jesus invites all of us on an adventure of loving one another. Are you in?

Who around you can you love and serve this week?

Jesus, please give me a heart of love for others. Show me ways to love and serve those around me this week.

You can read about loving others in John 13:31–35.

65

HE'S LISTENING

Can a mother forget her nursing child? Can
she feel no love for the child she has borne?
But even if that were possible, I would not
forget you! See, I have written your name on
the palms of my hands.

Isaiah 49:15–16

Have you ever wondered if God's really listening? Like,
doesn't He have bigger, more important things to do than
talk to us (a.k.a. running the universe)?

Just in case you've ever wondered if God hears you (or even cares),
imagine this: you're only two years old, and you're running outside
on a beautiful summer day. Suddenly, you trip and fall, stubbing
your big toe.

Screaming, you run home to your Mom.

Would she have looked at you, bored and yawning, and said, "Why are you bothering me with something as small as a stubbed toe? I'm busy! I have more important things to deal with right now."

No way! Likely, your Mom would have sprung into action: finding a Band-Aid, washing your toe off, getting you all fixed up. She would have received you with love.

The Bible tells us that God loves us like that, as a mom loves her own kids. Even if she could stop loving her kids (nearly impossible), God says He promises never to stop loving us. He's even written our names on the palms of His hands (Isaiah 49:15–16)!

Your heavenly Father cares for you, and He's listening.

How much does God love you?

Jesus, You promise to never leave me or forget me. Even my name is written on Your hands! Thanks for loving me that much.

You can read how much God loves you in Isaiah 49:13–18.

66
DOING THE IMPOSSIBLE

For I can do everything through Christ,
who gives me strength.

Philippians 4:13

*n*othing gets in the way of a mother robin, especially when she's building her nest.

In the middle of a storm, one mother robin landed on a slanted roof. Normal birds wouldn't choose a slanted, slippery roof as the place to build a home. But this mother robin had a plan: You see, she carried lots of dirt with her. In the rain, the dirt tuned into mud glue. With this mud glue, she carefully mixed together leaves and twigs, and there, in that pouring rain—on a very slanted and slippery roof—this tough mother robin built herself a brand new nest. Wow.

If you never give up, it's amazing what you can do! This is especially true if you have the God of the universe on your side. The Bible says you can do "everything through Christ, who gives [you] strength" (Philippians 4:13). Even in the toughest times—those that leave you discouraged, sad, or scared—you can overcome by leaning on God's amazing power (whose power lives inside of you!).

With God alive in you, you can do all things.

When have you gone through a tough situation? How did God help you keep going?

Jesus, situations can be tough or overwhelming. With Your help, though, I know I can do all things, even the impossible!

You can read about never giving up in Romans 5:3–4.

67
BEING FAMOUS

Think of yourselves the way Christ Jesus thought of himself. He had equal status with God but didn't think so much of himself that he had to cling to the advantages of that status no matter what. Not at all.

Philippians 2:6 (MSG)

Many of us want to be famous. The most famous person of all time? According to *Time* magazine, it's Jesus.

Jesus didn't seek fame though. Just look at the way He came to Earth: Born in a room full of smelly animals, He was laid in an animal trough. And no one but the stinky shepherds welcomed Him.

Growing up, His goal wasn't to become a celebrity. During His whole life, Jesus stayed focused on His big purpose—to follow whatever His Father told him to do. (In His Father's eyes, He was already famous.)

You may find that everyone around you is obsessed with becoming famous. Or following famous people. Flip the rules. Follow Jesus's example instead: stay focused on listening and obeying whatever your Father in heaven says.

And know that you're already famous in the eyes of the King of the universe.

※※※※

Why didn't Jesus care about becoming famous?

Jesus, while it's fun to follow celebrities, help me not to forget that living in Your kingdom—following Your amazing plans—is way more exciting than being famous.

You can read about Jesus coming to Earth in Luke 2:1–20.

68
GOD'S FAVORITE FRUIT

I chose you. I appointed you to go and produce lasting fruit.

John 15:16

What're your favorite fruits? Tart and crisp apples? Sweet and tangy clementines? Or even slices of cold, refreshing watermelon? With so many delicious kinds, it's hard to decide which are the best.

God has favorite fruit too. At all times, the Holy Spirit is busily at work in your heart: planting seeds, tending to, and growing orchards full of amazing fruit. Fruit like love, joy, peace, patience and kindness, and more. The most exciting thing for the Holy Spirit? Watching these fruits mature in you! You see, the Holy Spirit is

a master Gardener. He delights to see how He's changing your thinking, your attitudes, and your actions in the process of tending to and growing His fruit in you. Through His gardening and attentive care, He's making you become more like Christ, God's Son. Nothing gives your Gardener more joy than seeing you grow to be more like Jesus.

Today, what kind of fruit is your Gardener growing inside of you?

What fruit has the Holy Spirit been growing in you?

Jesus, thanks for Your fruit that grows inside of me! Help me grow in love and joy and peace today.

You can read about the fruit of the Spirit in Galatians 5:22–23.

69

SAYING GOODBYE

First, the believers who have died will rise
from their graves. Then, together with them,
we . . . will be caught up in the clouds to meet
the Lord in the air.

1 Thessalonians 4:16–17

Olivia was her Grandma's buddy. Each week, they played games, ate pizza, and told each other funny stories.

Grandma was dying of cancer. Their last night together at the hospital, Olivia sat by her grandmother's side. Grandma took Olivia's hand in hers. She told Olivia how much her eight-year-old granddaughter meant to her, that she'd miss her, and that one day they'd have a big reunion in heaven together.

"When we see each other that day, we'll never have to say goodbye again," said Grandma.

Saying goodbye to her grandmother was still hard. Olivia wanted her grandma to stay with *her*. It's normal to want to hold onto our loved ones, just as Olivia did. You see, God designed us for never-ending, never-stopping life—eternal life. We were not made for the pain and separation of death. We were not meant to say goodbye.

As followers of Jesus, though, we do have real hope: the promise that one day we will see our loved ones, without ever having to say goodbye again.

Have you ever lost a family member or friend?

Jesus, it hurts to say goodbye. Thanks for helping me when I'm hurting and for promising me that one day I will see my loved ones again.

You can read about being together—forever—with your family and friends in 1 Thessalonians 4:13–18.

70

EARTH CARETAKERS

Then God looked over all he had made,
and he saw that it was very good!

Genesis 1:31

$\mathcal{H}$ave you ever made something that you were extremely proud of—like an art project, a science experiment, or even a song you wrote?

When God created the world, He felt just like that. God was so proud of all He had made He said *everything* was good. And He really meant *everything*.

Everything God made gave His heart joy.

What made God proudest of all? That would be all of us! He made humans special—like Him. The Bible says, "God created human beings in his own image" (Genesis 1:27). Because we are like Him, He gave us the huge responsibility of taking care of the earth and everything in it—the oceans, rivers, and lakes; the forests and farmlands; and all the animals too!

Let's each do our part in protecting the world around us.

※※※※

What's one thing you can do to take care of the earth?

Jesus, everything You made in the world is amazing. Show me how to take care of the earth and the animals, as You've called me to do!

You can read the creation story in Genesis 1:24–31.

71

IT'S NOT ABOUT US

[God] breathed the word, and all the
stars were born.

Psalm 33:6

*I*f you lived five hundred years ago, you probably would have believed that Earth was the center of the universe, as most everyone else did. Crazy, right?

We now know that Earth orbits the sun, and the sun is ordinary. It's just one of one hundred thousand million stars in the Milky Way galaxy. Sometimes, though, we still act as if *we* are the center of the universe. We believe everything is about us.

But when we think about the stars, we wake up to the fact it's not.

The Bible tells us God spoke, and the stars were born. He even named each of the stars in our Milky Way, not to mention naming each of the stars in the two trillion other galaxies spread across the universe. Wow.

Knowing we live on a tiny planet, circling an ordinary star, in just one of two trillion galaxies helps us understand it's not all about us. In fact, that's very good news because it just so happens that the Creator who holds that entire universe together also loves us.

❧❧❧❧❧

What about our galaxy fascinates you—a favorite star or constellation?

Jesus, I'm amazed by the universe You created, with its two trillion galaxies! I can't wrap my mind around the size of our universe. And that's OK, because You're holding it all together, not me.

You can read how God created the stars in Psalm 33:6–15.

72

GOOD THINGS

For we are God's masterpiece. He has created us anew in Christ Jesus, so we can do the good things he planned for us long ago.

Ephesians 2:10

$\mathcal{T}$here once was a guy who didn't like Christians. He was absolutely obsessed with locking them up or getting them killed. One day, on his way to arresting them, he met Jesus, and everything changed. Instead of killing Christians, this guy started sharing about Jesus with everyone he met. God chose him to teach and preach to churches across the world. His Hebrew name was Saul, but you may know him by his Greek name, Paul—the apostle who wrote most of the New Testament.

God flipped Paul's passion from the wrong things to the right ones—God's dreams and purposes for him! Just as God chose Paul,

He's chosen you. The Bible says, "He has created [you] anew in Christ Jesus, so [you] can do the good things he planned for [you] long ago" (Ephesians 2:10).

Don't underestimate God's plans for you. If God can take someone like Paul—who made some huge mistakes—to share God's love, imagine what He's dreaming up for you!

What dreams has God placed on your heart?

Jesus, You've got big dreams for me, things You've been planning for me even before I was born! Show me how to use my gifts for Your good plans.

You can read Paul's story in Acts 9:1–9.

73

BELIEVING GOD'S PROMISES

God has given us eternal life, and this life is in his Son. Whoever has the Son has life.

1 John 5:11–12 (NIV)

Will I really go to heaven? is a question we may ask ourselves. If you've ever wondered about this, listen in to this true story. One day, two-year-old William went missing. His parents searched for him *everywhere*. You can imagine how joyful they were to find their toddler playing in a neighbor's backyard.

Afterward, William's mom began telling everyone the story of searching for William, and the toddler got confused.

"Mommy!" he cried. "Did you ever find me?"

"Of course, William!" she said, surprised and touched by his fear. She took him in her arms.

"See, you're with us now, and we'll make sure you always are." That calmed William because he believed her promise.

Just as William's mom promised him that he was safely home, the Bible promises that whoever believes in Jesus has a forever home with Him (1 John 5:13). Because the Bible is God's Word, we can trust its promises are true.

So, if you have a relationship with Jesus, you've got a heavenly home to look forward to!

What do you think heaven will be like?

Jesus, thanks for promising to prepare a place for me in heaven. It's comforting to know that I have a forever home with You.

You can read God's promise of forever life in 1 John 5:11–13.

74
FINDING FAULT

And why worry about a speck in your friend's
eye when you have a log in your own

Matthew 7:3

You're having the most amazing day at school until . . .
. . . you waltz into the bathroom and glance at yourself in the
mirror. To your horror, you discover a huge piece of spinach
wrapped around your front teeth.

Since eating that spinach at lunchtime—all through your history
class, study hall, and band practice—you've been parading around
with this ginormous piece of spinach in your teeth, for everyone to
see.

This isn't a true story. How often, though, do we tear apart the
tiniest flaws in others? Meanwhile, we don't see our own *bigger*
issues—problems that everyone else can clearly see. It's kind of like
having spinach in our teeth.

That's why Jesus tells us to deal with our own problems before criticizing anyone else. He says, "And why worry about a speck in your friend's eye when you have a log in your own? . . . First get rid of the log in your own eye; then you will see well enough to deal with the speck in your friend's eye" (Matthew 7:3, 5).

Before finding fault in someone else, let's fix ourselves.

✦✦✦✦✦✦

What's one way you can build others up today?

Jesus, help me build up and encourage others instead of tearing them down and criticizing them. No one is perfect—including me! Please give me a humble heart.

You can read Jesus's wise advice in Matthew 7:3–5.

75
THE RIGHT IMAGE

So God created human beings in his own image.
In the image of God he created them; male and
female he created them.

Genesis 1:27

*H*ere's a heart-breaking truth: More than half of girls today are unhappy with their image. They believe the lie that they're not good enough. And it's a crippling one. The Bible, though, teaches that we're made in God's image (Genesis 1:27). This means you mirror God! Your Creator is beautiful and glorious, and since you're made in His image, so are you!

Don't believe the lie that you're not good enough. Instead, embrace the amazing truth about yourself: You are beautiful and glorious, made in the very image of your Creator.

You're made in God's image—what's incredible about that truth?

Jesus, help me remember who I am and whose I am—Your girl! Made in Your image, I am beautiful and glorious, like You!

You can read about being created in God's image in Genesis 1:26–31.

76

PRAYER WARRIOR

[Jesus] lives forever to intercede with God on their behalf.

Hebrews 7:25

alling all prayer warriors!

Jesus, the King of universe, is seeking you. Your King prays for you, your family, and your friends, day and night—never stopping (Hebrews 7:25). And He's looking for someone just like you to join Him in this very important work: in the special role of prayer warrior.

If you choose to take on this special assignment, here's your mission: *Pray mighty prayers on behalf of your family, friends, and others. Prayers that encourage them. Protect them. Help them be all God created them to be.*

As prayer warriors, we don't always know how to pray. That's OK! We can just cry out, "Jesus, help," or "Daddy in heaven." Hearing us, the Holy Spirit will pray for our friends on our behalf (Romans 8:14–16, 26–27). Pretty awesome, right?

So, will you take on this special assignment? Know that if you do, you've been handpicked as a warrior by your King.

Will you take on the special assignment of *prayer warrior*?

Jesus, thanks for always praying for me. Show me how to pray courageously for my friends and family, just as You do.

You can read how to be a prayer warrior in James 5:13–18.

77

WARNING: LACKING COMMON SENSE

For the LORD gives wisdom.

Proverbs 2:6 (NIV)

*D*o we have what's called *common sense*? If you read warnings on products, you have to wonder. Here are two crazy examples.

On a hair dryer: Never use while sleeping. (If this sounds impossible to you, know it actually happened, and the person's bed caught on fire!)

On a washing machine: Do not put any person in this washer. (A college student jumped into the washer.)

The Bible has a book all about common sense (and if these warnings show us anything, it's that common sense is not so common!). The book of Proverbs shares tiny, bite-sized pieces of advice called *proverbs*.

Read these two amazing proverbs about friendship:

"As iron sharpens iron, so a friend sharpens a friend." (27:17). (We need each other to be the best we can be!)

"Wounds from a sincere friend are better than many kisses from an enemy" (27:6). (True friends are honest; enemies aren't.)

Do you want to get wise? Check Proverbs out. You'll discover dazzling jewels of wisdom if you listen carefully to its tiny proverbs.

How do you make wise choices?

Jesus, thanks for giving us an entire book about wisdom. Whatever choices I face today, help me choose wisely.

You can read some wise advice in Proverbs 3:5–8.

78

BACK TOGETHER AGAIN

The LORD is close to the brokenhearted.

Psalm 34:18

Have you learned the nursery rhyme Humpty Dumpty? It begins "Humpty Dumpty sat on a wall." Do you remember what happens next? Humpty Dumpty falls off the wall, breaking into many pieces. At the end of the rhyme, no one can "put Humpty Dumpty together again."

Sometimes we can feel a lot like Humpty Dumpty. Our hearts can be broken into many pieces from unkind words, being excluded, maybe even our own unwise choices. The Bible says that Jesus "is close to the brokenhearted; he rescues those whose spirits are crushed" (Psalm 34:18). Jesus is a great Healer, and He is the One who can heal all our hurts and brokenness.

Whenever you're feeling sad or lonely or confused, you can talk to Jesus. He loves listening to you. Sometimes He might help you think of someone to talk to about your problems. Or he might bring something happy into your day.

Watch for how He's going to "put you together again"!

Do you remember a time when your heart was hurting? Tell Jesus how you felt.

Jesus, thank You for being with me when I am sad, angry, or alone. I know that when my heart aches, Your heart breaks too.

You can read about your Healer in Psalm 34:17–19.

79

REAL LIFE

**I came so they can have real and eternal life,
more and better life than they ever dreamed of.**

John 10:10 (MSG)

Some animals have a hard shell for their skin. It has a funny name—an *exoskeleton*. And many funny-looking (kind of creepy) creatures have them—cockroaches. Tarantulas. Even lobsters and crabs. Sometimes these creatures shed their shells. What's left? The even bigger creature and the old shell. The shell, though, can look *exactly* like the creature. Until you get *real* up close. Then you find out real fast which one is empty—very dead . . . and which one is crawling toward you. Yikes.

You know what else can look the same? Going through the motions at church and having a relationship with Jesus. Here's the thing:

Many people read their Bibles. Go to church every week. Even sing some worship songs. (And all of these are great things!) And, yet, without a relationship with Jesus, even the best "church stuff" is like that leftover exoskeleton. On the outside, it looks like the real deal. But it's actually empty. (Dead.)

The amazing truth? God wants to be our Friend! He even *lives* inside our hearts. Now stop right there. Think about that—the God of the entire universe is *alive* inside of you. That truth is so amazing, in fact, it's hard to even wrap our minds around!

So, go to church. Praise and worship God. And read your Bible. (All those things are great ways to get to know God better.) But never forget this incredible truth: the God of the universe is housed—is alive—inside of you.

And, what's more? He'd like to be your forever Friend.

ᶻᶻᶻᶻᶻᶻ

What's the difference between just doing church stuff and having a relationship with Jesus?

Jesus, it's hard to understand how the God of the entire universe—You—can live inside of me. But I'm going to believe that incredible truth with all my heart.

You can read about God's amazing gift of life in John 10:10–11.

80

WITH YOU, ALWAYS

You are all around me, behind me and in front of me. You hold me safe in your hand. I'm amazed at how well you know me. It's more than I can understand.

Psalm 139:5–6 (NIrV)

*E*very morning, Julie's black lab puppy, Tucker, wakes her up, jumping on her bed, tail wagging. His chocolate brown eyes seem to ask Julie, Are you ready to play with me?

Throughout the day, Tucker won't leave Julie's side. He follows her into the bathroom as she brushes her teeth. He lies down at her feet at dinner. And he sits on her lap while she does her homework (he even tries to eat it—sometimes Julie wishes he would!).

Tucker is loyal to Julie.

In the Bible, King David talks about God's loyal love for us: "You are all around me, behind me and in front of me. You hold me safe in your hand" (Psalm 139:5 NIrV). God goes before us, behind us. He is with us and for us. He watches our every step.

So, when you're walking to the bus stop? You've got a Friend, right there beside you. And when you're doing your homework? Sitting with you is Jesus, helping you creatively solve problems. And when you're feeling afraid? God will keep you safe.

God promises to be with you, always.

God's love for you is *loyal*. What does that mean?

Jesus, whatever I'm doing or wherever I am, You'll go with me—You're my biggest fan. Thanks for always watching over me.

You can read about God's loyal love for you in Psalm 139:1–12.

81
NO MORE HIDING

The Lord God called . . . "Where are you?"

Genesis 3:9 (NIV)

When you were a little, did you ever disobey your parents—then run and hide?

That's exactly what Adam and Eve did after they ate the forbidden fruit in the garden of Eden. They felt guilty. Instead of facing God, they ran, hiding behind some trees.

"Where are you?" God called out to them (Genesis 3:9 NIV). As any friend would, God was trying to make things right with them again.

Just like Adam and Eve, sometimes we try to hide from God when we mess up, afraid God would stop loving us if He *really* knew what we had done.

God's love for us doesn't change. No matter if we're good or bad, performing the best or failing at everything, on the top or at the bottom. The fact is: we're His kids, and there's absolutely nothing that can separate us from His love.

Have you messed up? Don't hide. Go talk to Jesus. He'll be there, waiting for you—ready to show you just how much He loves you.

Have you ever tried to hide from God or the people you love? Why?

Jesus, whenever I feel embarrassed, sad, or ashamed, help me run to You instead of running away from You. Because no matter what, You will always love me.

You can read Adam and Eve's story in Genesis 3:1–9.

82

GOD'S SURPRISE

**Suddenly, their eyes were opened, and
they recognized him. And at that moment
he disappeared!**

Luke 24:31

Have you ever been ridiculously surprised? So much so that
you were left open-mouthed, in shock? Maybe you were
even blown away, almost to the point of falling over?

Two of Jesus's friends were dumbfounded and amazed, just like
that. But the day they experienced such joy, in fact, started out as
one of the lowest days in their lives. Three days earlier, Jesus had
been crucified. Not sure what to do, and incredibly sad and discouraged, they began walking. That's when a stranger approached
them. Amazed by His wisdom, they invited Him to continue walking, eventually inviting Him to dinner.

At dinner, God opened the two friends' eyes to recognize who was with them—it was Jesus! Immediately, Jesus disappeared. The two men, who probably fell off their chairs in shock, quickly recovered. With joy and amazement, they jumped to their feet and ran straight outside, telling the whole world Jesus was alive!

Now you've got to admit: That's probably one of God's best surprises. Ever.

If you had been the disciples in this story, what would you have done after you learned Jesus was alive?

Jesus, how amazing that You came back to life! You made it possible for all of us to live forever with You!

You can read about God's great surprise in Luke 24:13–34.

83

MISSING: GLOVES

**Your unfailing love, O Lord, is as vast
as the heavens. . . . You care for people
and animals alike.**

Psalm 36:5–6

The winter gloves kept disappearing.

Megan remembers the day her Mom confronted her about them. Every week before that day she'd gone to school with a new pair only to come home without them.

"Megan, you've got to be more responsible! This can't go on!"

Tears fell down Megan's cheeks. She wasn't losing her gloves, she said. She was giving them away to kids who couldn't afford them. And it was a cold winter.

Now in high school, Megan continues to give and serve; daily she mentors kids in an after-school program. She also volunteers at the local soup kitchen during the winter, handing out hot cocoa and coffee on cold winter nights.

Megan's heart reflects God's generous one. With Jesus in your heart, your heart mirrors God's too! Today, how can you show God's love through what you say and do?

※※※※※

What ways can you help or serve people (or pets!) in your community?

Jesus, show me ways to love and serve the people around me. Help me be generous, like You.

You can read about God's generous love in Psalm 36:5–10.

84

ONE HUNDRED YEAR CAMPING TRIP

Because of his faith [Abraham] made his
home in the land God had promised him.
Abraham was like an outsider in a strange
country. He lived there in tents.

Hebrews 11:9 (NIrV)

Have you ever gone camping? What an adventure. You get to build campfires, explore the woods, and—best of all—eat s'mores! But sleeping in a tent can be uncomfortable, especially on a rainy night. The next morning, you may wake up in a soggy sleeping bag. Yikes.

Most of us can "rough it" in a tent for a couple of days.

Imagine, though, sleeping in a tent for a hundred years. That's exactly what Abraham, one of the heroes of the Bible, did. When Abraham was seventy-five years old, God told him to leave his country, so Abraham packed up and traveled to a new land, living the rest of his life—until he was one hundred seventy-five years old—in tents. What an incredibly long camping trip.

Why did Abraham not mind camping out for one hundred years? Because he was excited about a heavenly home. God is readying a place for you too! A home in which you'll experience His love and joy, His beauty and goodness, His hope and peace, forever and ever. A place where you will no longer be sad, or lonely, or afraid. A place where you will celebrate with Him for all eternity.

It'll be like coming home after a really long camping trip.

Why did Abraham not grumble about going camping for one hundred years?

Jesus, thank You for my home—a place to eat, sleep, and do homework. My home here is such a gift. I'm also excited about my forever home that You're preparing for me!

You can read about God's new home for you in Revelation 21:3–5.

85

MEET YOUR GUEST

**I will talk to the Father, and he'll provide you another
Friend so that you will always have someone with you.
This Friend is the Spirit of Truth.**

John 14:16–17 (MSG)

*I*f someone visits your house for a week, your parents will likely
want to know *everything* about this person. (They are wise.)
In the Bible, Jesus himself has provided a description of the
new person moving in to—or who has already moved in to—your
house!

That's right! You have a new houseguest. Here are three important
things Jesus thought you should know to get acquainted:

1. **He helps out.** Your parents will be very pleased to know
    your new guest isn't messy. (Whew.) In fact, your friend's
    entire purpose is to help you (John 14:16–17)! (One of His

names is *Helper*.) His biggest joy? Making you be all God created you to be!

2. **He gives great advice.** Are you struggling to make a good choice? You can go to your friend for wisdom (John 14:26). (Another name of His is *Counselor*.)

3. **He's staying forever.** Once you invite your friend in, He's never leaving (John 14:16). It's true. If He were annoying? A big problem, indeed! But your friend is hard not to like; He wants what's best for you. He's always watching out for you. He will never fail you. (He's for you.)

So, who's this amazing new guest? The Holy Spirit—one of the three Persons of God. When you invite Jesus into your heart and life, the Holy Spirit moves in. Permanently.

Your heart, in fact, becomes His home address.

※※※※

What's amazing about your new houseguest—the Holy Spirit?

Jesus, thanks for sending Your Holy Spirit to live inside of me. He's awesome—a Helper, Counselor, and Friend. I'll listen to Him!

You can read about the Holy Spirit in Acts 1:4–5, 8–9.

86
HEART STUFF

Above all else, guard your heart,
for everything you do flows from it.

Proverbs 4:23 (NIV)

*D*id you know that your heart pumps about two thousand gallons of blood each day? That means every day your heart creates enough energy to drive a car twenty miles. Wow. And in your lifetime? You create enough energy to drive to the moon and back. That's pretty amazing! A healthy heart can do incredible things, but if your heart fails, your whole body shuts down.

The Bible talks a lot about your "spiritual heart." Just like your physical heart, your spiritual heart keeps you up and running, except the spiritual heart doesn't pump blood. No! The spiritual heart is that central place inside of you where you think, feel, and make choices.

Because it's so important, the Bible tells us to "guard [our] heart[s]" (Proverbs 4:23 NIV). So, stay away from trouble. Don't talk badly about others. And do the right thing. By listening to God and doing what He says, you'll keep your spiritual heart in great shape.

✺✺✺✺✺

Share a few ways you can keep your spiritual heart as healthy as it can be.

Jesus, teach me to listen to You and do what You say, so that I can avoid trouble.

You can read about guarding your heart in Proverbs 4:20–27.

87

WAS JESUS EVER LONELY?

A time is coming and in fact has come when you will be scattered, each to your own home. You will leave me all alone. Yet I am not alone, for my Father is with me.

John 16:32 (NIV)

You can have tons of friends on social media but still feel lonely. Why? God created us for close, face-to-face inter-actions, and if we don't get that, we can get lonely. Even if we're connecting with a bazillion friends digitally.

Jesus knows what it's like to be lonely. He was rejected, laughed at, pushed aside. Even his best friends left Him all alone on the absolute worst day of His life, the day He died on the cross. Yet, He always had one Friend who was always there for Him—His Father.

He told His disciples: "You will leave me all alone. Yet I am not alone, for the Father is with me" (John 16:32 NIV).

Through His death and resurrection, Jesus made it possible for us to be friends with His Father too! We still live in a broken, imperfect world. At times, we'll still feel lonely. But our heavenly Father promises to watch over us, to guide us, and to always be there for us, and in fact, He's overjoyed just to spend time with us.

Even if you're lonely, know you're never alone.

When have you felt lonely?

Jesus, whenever I feel sad, rejected, or alone, help me to remember that You are always with me.

You can read about a time Jesus felt lonely in Mark 14:43–50.

88

SPACESHIP PRAYER

I will do whatever you ask in my name, so that the Father may be glorified in the Son.

John 14:13 (NIV)

Five-year-old Noah wanted a Lego space rocket for Christmas. While he was shopping with Mom, Noah found the *exact* one he wanted. A shiny silver spaceship, complete with one hundred Lego pieces. "Mommy, I want this one. Pleeeease!" he begged and whined. Mom said, "We'll see," and took him home.

Sure enough, among the presents he opened on Christmas morning was the little space rocket. Noah was excited—until his older brother said, "You were silly to push for that one. Mom already bought you a much bigger space rocket—with *three hundred* Lego pieces—but when you begged for that littler one, she swapped it out!"

Noah's Lego spaceship looked less exciting.

Sometimes we're like that with God. We pray about a specific need and tell God *exactly* how He should answer. We beg and plead—and God may even give us what we ask for. But He may have had something bigger and better in mind.

So pray for God's plans for your life. Make room for God's big and beautiful ideas too. He could surprise you with something more amazing than what you would have asked for.

꓅꓅꓅꓅

What's the best gift you've ever received?

Jesus, You usually have better plans for me than I do for myself. Help me pray big prayers and make room in my heart for Your bigger and better plans and gifts!

You can read about prayer in John 15:7–14.

89

BIG CATS AND COURAGE

When Daniel learned that the law had been signed, he went home and . . . prayed three times a day, just as he had always done, giving thanks to his God.

Daniel 6:10

*D*id you know that you can hear a lion roar up to five miles away? With strength, power, and speed to match that mighty roar, it's no wonder the lion is called the "king of the jungle."

Understanding how fierce lions are shows us the amazing courage of Daniel in the Bible. When Daniel was honored by King Darius, the other leaders got jealous. They schemed, plotted, and figured out a sneaky plan to kill him. They wrote a law saying you could pray only to the king (knowing Daniel prayed to God alone). The punishment? A trip to the lions' den.

After hearing about this law, Daniel had a tough choice: he could listen to God or avoid the lions' den. Incredibly, Daniel went home, kneeled down, and prayed as usual, leading the evil leaders to throw him to the lions.

We know this story has a good ending (God miraculously protected Daniel). But our hero Daniel didn't. He believed the God who created the lion could shut its mouth, but he had no idea God would rescue him from the lions' den.

Daniel chose to be obedient to God, no matter the cost.

When have you chosen to do the right thing—even if it was a tough decision?

Jesus, give me the courage to be like Daniel—to follow You, no matter the cost.

You can read the story of Daniel in the lions' den in Daniel 6.

90

GIRL AFTER GOD'S HEART

The LORD doesn't see things the way you see
them. People judge by outward appearance,
but the LORD looks at the heart.

1 Samuel 16:7

Betty Cuthbert didn't laugh the loudest. Or talk the most. She
was rather shy. So it may surprise you that she was a champion. As a teenager, she won three gold medals in sprinting
at the Olympics!

Soon after, she got injured. Everyone—including Betty—thought
her running days were over. Then, one night, she heard God's
voice. He told her not to give up running. After thinking about it,
she said to God, "OK, you win. I'll run again."

She didn't just run again; she *won* gold at the next Olympics. No
matter how challenging her circumstances, Betty wouldn't give
up: God had given her the heart of a champion. Champions don't
always look or act the way we expect. When the prophet Samuel

saw Jesse's oldest and strongest son, he said to himself, "There's the next king of Israel: he's tall, handsome, and strong!"

God told Samuel he had gotten it all wrong, "People judge by outward appearance, but the LORD looks at the heart" (1 Samuel 16:7). So, who did God choose as Israel's next king? Jesse's youngest, smallest son—David—who cared for his father's sheep. Compared to his seven brothers, he didn't look like a champion. But David was after God's own heart (Acts 13:22).

God is still searching for champions like David . . . like Betty. They may not be the loudest, strongest, or most popular. But He's looking for people who love Him. People who want to serve Him.

Girls after God's own heart.

Why did God choose David to be king over his older, stronger brothers?

Jesus, help me to be a girl after Your heart. Thanks for caring about what's on the inside of me. Teach me how to follow You with everything I've got!

You can read David's story in 1 Samuel 16:1–13.

APPENDIX

How Can I Be Friends with God?

*L*et's begin with the most amazing truth of all time: The God of the universe loves you. In fact, God has *always* loved you (even before you existed!). And God will never stop loving you.

The heartbreaking thing, though? Because of the sin in our hearts, we run away from God. Sin is anything that keeps us from God (and many times, it involves making poor choices, disobeying, or not doing what's right). God *hates* being apart from us, the kids He created.

God created a rescue plan so that we could be close to Him: sending His Son Jesus to Earth to show us just how much He loved us. Jesus took away our sins by dying on a cross and coming back to life again. He made it possible for us to be friends with God—living forever with Him (John 3:16).

If you'd like to have a personal relationship with Jesus, you can ask God into your heart and life right now!

Dear God, I want to be near to You.
Thank you for sending Your Son Jesus
to die on the cross for my sins. I'm
sorry for my sins. Please come into
my heart and life; I want to love and
follow You with my whole heart.
In Jesus's name, amen.

Welcome to God's big family. Now go celebrate, maybe inviting your friends and family to join in the fun—they'll likely be excited about your decision to follow Jesus too! Then, connect with a church where you can find friendship as you grow in your faith.

Finally, don't forget: God loves you. God has always loved you. And God will never stop loving you (Romans 8:38–39).